COW COUNTRY COOKBOOK

COW COUNTRY COOKBOOK

DAN CUSHMAN

ILLUSTRATED BY CHARLIE RUSSELL
FOREWORD BY MAX EVANS

CLEAR LIGHT PUBLISHERS
SANTA FE

Clear Light Publishers
823 Don Diego
Santa Fe, New Mexico 87501

International Standard Book Number:
ISBN 0-940666-18-9
Library of Congress Catalogue Number:
91-58826

First Printing

Designed by Irving Warhaftig
Printed in the U. S. A. by Baker Johnson Book Printing & Binding

CONTENTS

Here's hoping the worst end of your trail
is behind you
That Dad Time be your friend from
here to the End
And sickness nor sorrow dont
find you

CMRussell 1926

FOREWORD

BY MAX EVANS

Dan Cushman is, indeed, a fine writer of humorous truths. Here in his *Cow Country Cookbook* you get a two-for-one bargain: cow pasture, line-camp, ranch headquarters gourmet recipes along with good-natured writing to fulfill both the gustatory and big smile appetites.

Dan Cushman is a writer whose work I've read and admired for a long time. If he doesn't have a cult following, he certainly should have, and you can put me at the top of the list.

One of life's most lasting memories from my youth while working on various cow ranches, was pinto beans. We had boiled beans, re-fried beans, baked beans, salt pork beans, chile beans, brisket beans, and yes, finally that greatest of cautious delicacies "bean pie." Most of this is covered here by Cushman, as well as his Fried Peach Pie.

My first experience with dried fruit desserts was in a line camp where my old cowboy uncle, Slim, rubbed the insides of a Dutch oven with a piece of sowbelly (slab bacon) then threw in some dried peaches, flour, sugar, and water, covered it with some biscuit dough, and placed it on the iron stove. When I asked him what he had just made, he looked at me as if I were a rotted fence post that needed to be replaced, and said, "Hell, that's cowboy cobbler." Whatever he, or Cushman, called it, I never tasted anything better.

Decades later when I was a starving artist in Taos, New Mexico, Slim stopped by for a visit (a six-month visit). One day he asked my wife, Pat, if she'd mind fixing us a cowboy cobbler. My memory bank clicked in, and I immediately suggested that we'd appreciate him coming up with one of his creations. After we finished our delicious boiled beans with ham, we all three sure enjoyed the dessert.

Here in these pages you can find how to treat yourself to Strong-arm Steak, real sourdough bread, Son-of-a-Bitch Stew, Firehole Beans, and Wildcat Pie washed down with homemade Chokecherry Wine.

Don't forget to tell your friends about this cowboy culinary saga and the first-rate writer who put it together. They'll love you for the favor.

INTRODUCTION

As a young fellow of high school age I had a job of sorts with *The Mountaineer,* our Big Sandy, Montana, weekly paper (we had a good view of the Bearpaw Mountains). I was paid two dollars per week for setting type and running proofs around town (population 850). It was all I earned.

One day, seated with a view of the street—solid dried gumbo with ruts—and a view of the lumberyard, a bright cream-yellow roadster pulled up, and a tall, fine-looking man of about thirty-five got out; he saw the *Mountaineer* sign and came in. He introduced himself as Herbert Peet, state editor of the *Great Falls Tribune,* Montana's best statewide newspaper.

Big Sandy had a correspondent, but he was the superintendent of schools, generally gone most of the summer, when crops were growing; and even on the job he seemed to think that the educational establishment, which was a good one, was more important than how many trainloads of cattle? how much wheat? and what about the oil-drilling rig south of the Bear Paws? At any rate, I had been the one sending in the news, so I was the one Mr. Peet was looking for.

Mr. Peet left a long yellow sheet of instructions—it was printed on both sides—telling how to be a news writer for the *Tribune*. One item in particular struck me with force: "If a dog bites a man, that's not news, unless the bite is serious; but if a man bites a dog, that's news!" My brother Beecher, who was a student at the University of Missouri School of Journalism, really scoffed at that one! Especially the part about "unless the bite is serious." It spoiled what was at all events an old saw in the profession. (I imagine Mr. Peet was afraid some correspondent would have somebody bitten by a rabid wolfhound, and not send it in.) At any rate, Beech was not there at the time I read it, and it was my journalistic epiphany: the scales had fallen from my eyes; I had become Hildy Johnson in *The Front Page*.

It was a great spot for a *Tribune* correspondent. Big Sandy led the state, and sometimes the country, in cattle. In 1916 it had led the nation as a shipper of wheat. How were the crops? The paper was always willing to report on crops, the conditions on Lone Tree Bench, the Maris River, and on most work-a-day doings of agricultural folk. Soon the Big Sandy correspondent was making as much as a store clerk, while living at home for nothing and being courted by people who wanted to see their names in print. But then Christmas would come.

It was a merry time of year, but no longer did the wheat trucks and wagons roll; or the cattle, wall-eyed and frightened at what was happening, gather, fragrant and mooing, at the stockyards. The supplies had all been purchased, big tandem wagons loaded to the tops with ranch supplies and driven away, all gone, bound for places perhaps 90 miles away, where the cattle wintered. I was suddenly down to writing about basketball games, listing vital statistics, and the like.

Now, cowboys "wintering their saddles in town," and plenty of camp cooks, sat all day in Pep Williford's pool hall, playing poker, nursing dollar stacks of chips. Old-time ranchers, wealthy and retired, lived in Billy Snow's Montana Hotel, and looked forward to the vacations of the Japanese and Chinese owners of our two chief restaurants, whereupon some favored camp cook took over in the kitchens, and one heard tales of this and that food, generally the sourdough camp biscuits soon to be. Cowboys and cooks (and the author of this book) favored Jim Wallace's Feed Stable, a block square, reminding one of some frontier fort, with open ground and watering tank in the middle; roofed shelter for horses; closed and unclosed shelters for hay and similar supplies; and a large, low building containing blacksmithing equipment, two kitchens with coal ranges, a bar, card tables, and a wall lined with hay-filled bunks, three tiers, where men slept while games went on—poker, blackjack, solo; it was all very friendly and fragrant under the smoke from pipes and Bull Durham. Mama said I was sure to get lousy, but I never did.

There was a good deal of free-lance cooking that took place at the Feed Stable. People who weren't cowboys were likely to be range cooks, or had great tales to tell of men who were. "Get old Good-Eye to tell you about his Six-Shooter Steak. You have to pound it with the butt of a six-shooter." And the boys would argue. So I thought, why not a long piece on range and ranch cooking? I certainly had plenty of sources, both practitioners and consumers.

I collected material and wrote my piece, a long one, and sent it off. Would the *Tribune* print it as a single, multi-column feature? Would it be used as a *series*, or in a *special section* on Sunday, maybe even carried over several Sundays?

I waited, but nothing happened. My magnum piece was never acknowledged, and I was shrewd enough in the ways of the craft not to ask about it. My camp-cook recipes were not "on the hook," and that was that.

Advice to writers: never throw anything away. I kept the carbons of my cookbook. The journal of Henry David Thoreau was found in his family attic, rain-stained but legible for future generations. Like Thoreau's book, my *Cow Country Cookbook* was found in the family attic years later. I read it, expanded it from sources as remote as the

Hudson's Bay Company (which sent cooking instructions with its factors in the wilderness), and published it in 1967 under the title *Dan Cushman's Cow-Country Cookbook*.

The book did real well. Particularly out West. My greatest satisfaction came when the Musselshell Valley Historical Museum, of Round-up, Montana, asked to reprint some favored recipes in its book *Old Time Chuck*, and ended by saying, " We are indebted to Dan Cushman for most of the above material." And although the *Great Falls Tribune* never printed my camp-cook recipes, the directors of Montana's leading daily were kind enough to let me use, gratis, a series of pen and ink sketches—most of them the smaller action sketches of larger drawings—which had been commissioned by them from Charlie Russell, the cowboy artist, in the early years of the century.

Charlie was a Missourian of good family who longed early for the Cowboy West, and came in 1874, at sixteen, to start at the very bottom, in the cowboy view of things—tending sheep. Soon, though, Charlie was cowboying full-time in Judith Basin, one of the queen areas which had recently seen the last of the wild buffalo. During the terrible winter of 1887, it was his sketch of a lone, starving steer, head down against a blizzard, that started him off as a cowboy-illustrator. Eventually, he became one of the great ones, a real legend.

After it had been out of print for twenty-five years, Harmon

Houghton and Marcia Keegan of Clear Light Publishers, in Santa Fe, responded to the first edition of my cookbook, and why not? New Mexico seemed to have sent a large number of its cowboys north with the trail herds—men who stayed north in spite of a cold which caused cottonwood trees to explode from locked moisture in the wintertime. The speech of the Bear Paws is, to this day, notably softened by the southwestern accent. It's good to see the recipes back in print—and with even more of Charlie Russell's illustrations than before. I think Charlie would like it too.

Dan Cushman
Great Falls, Montana

STEAKS

RARE, MEDIUM, WELL-DONE

According to legend, westerners ate their beefsteaks rare. "Just knock the horns off and run him in," the cowboy was supposed to have said. More in line with the facts was the old story of the cowboy who dropped in at the Chequamegon Cafe, grazing place of the copper kings, while taking in the high life of Butte. He ordered a T-bone, which was served to him very thick and rare. "Would you like me to bring you the Bordelaise sauce?" asked the waitress when she observed his hesitation after the first knife cut.

"Gosh no," he answered, "bring the liniment. I think we may be able to save this one."

There is a trick to getting steak rare without leaving it raw, and well-done without utterly killing it. Much more difficult is trying to rescue one when it has just turned medium. Also, there are people who

1

ask for their steak medium-rare, medium-well, etc. Acknowledging at the outset that the odds are against you, it is generally less of a gamble to take the steak off a bit before it has reached what seems to be the proper stage. If a steak is hot and steaming all the way through, it will continue to cook for a while on the hot platter. Anyhow, it's a shame to ruin a fine steak by turning it to blotter on the griddle.

On the other hand, a rare steak doesn't mean raw. You may time the steaks, a highly fallible procedure because temperatures and thicknesses vary. Some cooks observe the fat. Fat which was dense white will turn yellowish and translucent when it starts to fry out. When the thickest fat is translucent, the steak has actually started to cook all the way through. Take it off without delay. Another sign to watch is the shrinkage of meat away from the bone. When steak touches griddle, bone and flesh meet at an even plane. Very soon the bone will stand up thicker than the meat. With a little practice a glance at the fat and at the bone will tell you how far the cooking has proceeded.

Camp cooks expecting to be supplied with tough beef were seldom disappointed. Although the roundup might produce an abundance of grass-fat steers, no boss would have them butchered for his employees. He wasn't against prime meat, but he wanted it to come from a maverick, a stray. Fat mavericks weren't too plentiful, hence the animal chosen for camp was likely to be of a quality best suited to prolonged stewing. The cowboys cried out for steak.

Some cooks cut tough steaks very thin and fried them quickly. This helped, but not very much. A better method was to cut them thick and pound them. There were many preferences for pounding—a dull butcher knife, the back of a cleaver, a chain flail, even the side of a dish. But the favorite among old-time cooks was the six-shooter, the standard Peacemaker Colt, single action, .45-caliber, 7½-inch barrel.

Truly, the six-shooter was versatile. It was twice used as a tool to once as a weapon. Fighting men often preferred the newer patent pistols with their hinged mechanisms to speed reloading. Out on the range the Peacemaker with its solid frame was highly regarded. It took terrible abuse without misalignment. Staples were pried from fence posts with its forward sight and hammered back with its butt. It was used to reset horseshoe nails, its pointed butt being a good substitute for a farrier's hammer, and its barrel was an ideal anvil for rivetting harness gear. Its handle made a shoemaker's last when boots needed

SIX-SHOOTER STEAK

**2 full-cut round steaks
1 teaspoon peppercorns
1 cup flour
1 cup lard
salt**

3

emergency half-soling. Its length served as a ruler, being 12 inches overall. Lacking brace and bit, the empty cartridges cut holes, and the bullets served as pencils for numbering claim corners, filling out notices of preemption, and painstakingly drawing letters to the folks back home.

Cooks favored a six-shooter for pounding tough beefsteak because it had good weight and balance, the barrel fit the hand, and the butt, ending in a wedge of steel, was shaped to bruise the meat, to pulp and tenderize it, without punching holes all the way through. (Cooks were also said to use the ammunition, pulling the bullets to get at the gunpowder as a substitute for pepper. Black powder was sometimes sprinkled on raw beef and taken for stomach complaint, but cooks had better use for cartridges at five cents each than as a source of condiment. They got pepper in sacks, whole, and crushed it as needed.)

To prepare a good six-shooter steak, start by pulverizing the peppercorns. Don't grind them, just crush them on a slab of hardwood. Brush them into the cup of flour; any fragments left will be picked up when the steak is pounded. Cut the round steaks into the desired sizes. Do not trim off the fat. Using the butt of a six-shooter, pound them while sprinkling them lightly with flour and pepper. Don't hammer. Merely lift the gun and let it fall. Its weight—2 pounds loaded—will be sufficient. And don't work them down too thin. They are best

4

reduced to about two-thirds of their original thickness. Heat a heavy iron skillet or griddle. Melt the lard, and when it is hot enough to smoke, fry the steaks a few at a time, browning on both sides and setting aside in a warm pan while they are still red in the middle. Salt them. Cover the pan and keep it hot but not sizzling. The redness will fade after 3 or 4 minutes, and your genuine, old-time six-shooter steaks will go to the table done through, tender and delicious.

5

FANCY SIX-SHOOTER STEAK

2 full-cut round steaks, thick
1 teaspoon peppercorns
1 cup flour
3 tablespoons Worcestershire
  sauce
1 cup lard
salt

Few range cooks had anything as fancy as Worcestershire sauce, in those days generally referred to just as Lea & Perrins. Cooks with the freight outfits which stopped at the army posts and towns along the road were able to keep better supplied. Worcestershire not only added flavor but served as a tenderizer because of the vinegar it contained.

Pound the thick steaks with flour and pepper as in the foregoing recipe. When each is finished, sprinkle it with Worcestershire sauce. Stack the steaks one on the other and allow them to cure for ½ hour. Melt lard in a covered skillet or Dutch oven and fry until browned while still raw in the middle. Salt, cover tightly, and set off the heat. By the time the skillet is cool, the steaks will be done all the way through and a gravy will be formed which delicately coats each of them.

Out on the range fresh vegetables were hard to come by. Even at the home ranch they were scarce. Cattle ranchers didn't go much for gardening. A big-time rancher might not grow so much as one potato. Everything except beef was hauled from town, perhaps 150 miles away. Wild onions could be found growing all over the prairie early in the summer, but cooks thought gathering them was digger's work and demeaning. It helped when homesteaders started arriving. Cattlemen didn't object to homesteaders so much until they started registering their own brands and burning them on the sides of mavericks. Homesteaders almost always had a few vegetables to trade for a piece of beef, and cooks drove their wagons miles off course to get them. Turnips particularly thrived on freshly broken sod, and formed the chief ingredient, with beef, in a Dutch-Oven Steak.

Pound the steaks with flour. Pepper, and fry in a medium-hot Dutch oven. Chop the onions and dice the turnips. If wild onions are used, chop them fine. Put the onions and turnips evenly over the meat, sprinkle with salt, pour in water, cover tightly, and cook over a medium heat. Keep close watch and serve just as the liquid is exhausted and the steaks start once again to fry.

DUTCH-OVEN STEAK

5 pounds chuck steak
1/2 teaspoon black pepper
1 cup flour
1/2 cup water
1 cup lard
1 bunch green onions
2 large turnips
1 teaspoon salt

KANSAS CITY T-BONE

T-bone steaks, thick
marrow or suet
salt and pepper

This is the real, old-fashioned restaurant T-bone steak. By western tradition a Kansas City T-Bone had to be "so big a hound couldn't drag it off the plate." It had to come from a three year old at the very least. In the early days it was more likely to come from a four year old, or even a five year old. When an animal is fat off the grass, and its meat aged properly, which means for six weeks or more, such maturity is all to the good.

Today, very little real beefsteak is sold. Most of the steaks sold today come from long yearlings, animals less than two years old, which in the cow country of yesteryear would have been called baby beef. Compared with mature beef it is tender, but tasteless. A few ranchers still hold some of their steers until they attain the classic size, but chiefly for their own use. A real old-fashioned T-bone steak was expected to fill an 11 by 14-inch platter. These days, one sees "T-bones" being sold which measure no more than 4 by 7 inches. Even for baby beef this is too small. They are not T-bones at all, but trimmed rib steaks. Today, the largest steak of top quality one is likely to find will come from a three year old, and it will take some looking. If your market has nothing of the proper size, try a wholesaler doing business with the better restaurants. It may be you will be asked to buy the whole loin, but it can be frozen and the price will be lower.

Have your steaks cut 1 inch thick. Steaks of 1¼ inches may be all right for broiling, but they are too thick for the best results fried. Trim and leave out to warm at room temperature. Steak is best fried in marrow. Marrow can be saved from round steaks, or your butcher can get a supply by sawing the bones lengthwise when preparing soupbones or shank stew. If no marrow is available, use suet. Put marrow or suet on a griddle and wait for it to fry out and the oil to spread until it covers an area equal to the steak.

The griddle, incidentally, should be the heaviest you can find. A large steak, even if it's warmed beforehand, will pull a great deal of heat from the iron. A small griddle makes it impossible to obtain an even heat. Restaurant-size griddles, which often are just the tops of the ranges, will hardly fit a home kitchen, but might be great at the barbecue. Restaurant supply houses can furnish any size of griddle one might want, but for outdoor use try an ironworks or a welding shop. A griddle suitable for the outdoors can be cut from scrap at a fraction of the store price.

Wipe the steak on both sides with a damp cloth and put directly on what is left of the fried-out marrow or suet. Cover with a flat tin or lid, or you may wish to use a wooden slab. Allow the steak to do most of its cooking before turning it over. If the steak is to cook for 4 minutes, then cook it for 3 minutes on the first side and 1 minute on the other.

Turn it to a fresh place on the griddle, a spot newly shining with oil. Cover it again or not as you prefer. Salt just before removing from the heat. Pour a few drops of water on the griddle where it fried, wait for it to make thick, brown bubbles, and scrape up with one or two strokes of a spatula. Allow this to dribble over the steak.

Pep Williford, the western ballplayer and bartender, used to tell about the big-time Kansas City gambler found one morning lifeless on the sidewalk, the suspected victim of foul play. A medical examination, however, proved this not to be the case. His body bore no marks of bullets, no cuts or contusions. Nor was there evidence of fatal disease, only a pronounced emaciation.

"Why, this man," said the examining physician, "died of nothing in the world except starvation."

Yes, it was true. After a long run of poor luck he had found himself at the point where all he could get cuffo in the restaurants were pork and beans, beef stew, hamburger, pig hocks, and sauerkraut, while his position as a high roller demanded that he be seen eating only the quality cuts.

The story has to be true. Big gamblers feared death less than the thought of being deemed small-time, white-chip, or chippy. Their

DEMI-MONDE TENDERLOIN STEAK WITH MUSHROOMS

2 tenderloin steaks
1 cup mushrooms
1 tablespoon lard
1 tablespoon flour
1/8 pound butter
salt and pepper
1 slice toasted bread
parsley
French endive

shoes were likely to be bench-made by Stacy Adams. "St. James Infirmary," that national anthem of the segregated district, contained these words of a Kansas City gambler:

When I die I want to be buried in great fashion,
on my head a Stetson hat.

True, true, the Stetson was preferred, although some liked the extra-soft Borsalino, or the Dobbs velour. Gamblers affected a rumpled appearance while garbed in the best wools, personally tailored. Most of them fastidiously smoked long, thin panatela cigars, rather than the fat, clubhouse shapes. Cigarette smokers were likely to roll their own. In the old West, tailor-mades were looked down on. Tailor-mades were the badge of a cheap hustler. Besides, the hand-rolled cigarette would go out when laid down, and not keep burning and leave a brown streak across the top chip. Arising about eleven in the morning, gamblers perhaps had coffee at a saloon lunch counter, but their supper at eight, midnight, or three a.m. was taken at the best restaurant. The best on their own side of the tracks, that is. Oysters were much in favor, but the traditional preference of gamblers was the tenderloin steak.

Choose tenderloins from mature beef. A three year old with white fat and dark red flesh is ideal. Brighter red is likely to be baby beef or beef improperly aged. Tenderloins can be of several diameters depending on where in the strip they are cut, and all are good. Two tenderloins about 5 inches in diameter and 1 inch thick are just about right.

Allow the tenderloins to reach room temperature. Make sure the heavy iron griddle is smoking hot. Polish it with a clean, damp cloth. Put on the lard, stiff and white from the bucket. Allow the lard to melt and assume hot patterns. Put on the tenderloins. After 10 seconds move them to a fresh, greased place on the griddle. Then cover with a light tin.

Have a small frying pan hot and ready. Cut the butter into it. While the butter is melting on a very hot part of the stove, shake a cupful of damp, cold button mushrooms in a paper bag containing the flour. When the butter has stopped foaming and has started to brown, put in the mushrooms. Shake the frying pan from time to time. Allow the tenderloins to fry until almost the proper point on the first side, turn over for a quick brazing. Place them on a large platter. Sprinkle ground pepper on the griddle, pour on a little water, let foam briefly, scrape up with a spatula, and dribble over the meat. Remove the mushrooms, leaving the excess butter to be used later, and heap on one edge of the platter. Using the fingers, sprinkle salt and pepper lightly. You may wish to grind a pinch of salt with pepper and throw it at the meat.

Some cooks maintain this brightens the flavor. Pour the remaining butter on the griddle and fry a slice of lightly toasted bread on one side. It won't actually fry, but it will lie and become impregnated by the smoking butter. Quarter the toast and arrange around the platter, garnish with parsley and French endive. Serve with a tureen of sauce, the recipe for which follows.

Choose a soupbone not too denuded of good, red meat. Half cover with cold water, add salt, peppercorns, bay leaf, and cloves, slowly bring to a boil, and simmer for about 5 hours. Remove the bone, strain, and let stand until cold. Lift off the grease. Add the green onions chopped fine, butter, and chopped marrow; boil until the amount is reduced to about 4 cups. Strain. Make a thin paste of flour and cold water and add this little by little, resisting the temptation to form anything as thick as a gravy. Add just enough flour to give the sauce a little weight. Store in the refrigerator and serve warm, as needed.

STEAK SAUCE

4-pound soupbone
6 whole cloves
water
1 bay leaf
1 teaspoon salt
1 bunch green onions
1 tablespoon peppercorns
1/3 cup butter
flour as needed
1/3 cup marrow

15

STRONGARM STEAK
ALSO CALLED OLD ENGLISH STEAK

1 round steak, cubed
salt and pepper
suet

Although this is a pounded steak, it has very little resemblance to Six-Shooter Steak, or any other pounded steak for that matter.

Have a round steak cut a full 2½ inches thick. Divide it into cubes. Flatten each cube by striking it repeatedly with the face of a cleaver. When finished, the steaks will be rounded patties about 4 inches across and ¾ inch thick. Render pure leaf suet in a heavy pan until it contains ½ inch of oil, very hot. Fry the steaks a few at a time. Overcooking will be very easy, so rescue when still red in the middle and place in a warming oven. Sometimes called Old English Steak, this was a great favorite with the Cousin Jacks—the Cornish and Welsh who came in numbers to the early western hardrock camps.

16

Ribbon Steak

4 pounds round steak, cut thin
8 small onions
1 tall can milk
4 cups bread crumbs
1 cup olive oil
salt and pepper

Peel the onions and boil them in salted water. Cut the steak in strips about ½ inch across and 6 inches long. Save the bones and fry slowly in a heavy skillet. Remove the bones and discard when the marrow falls out. Dip the beef strips in canned milk, in crumbs, and in canned milk again. Add the olive oil to the marrow and fry the ribbons a few at a time. The canned milk may get thick with bread crumbs, so more milk and a little water can be added. When the steak is fried and stored in a warming oven, make a mixture of the onions and the crumb-filled milk used for the dipping, pour in the pan, and allow to boil until thick and buttery-brown in color. Pour over the steak. Salt and pepper to taste.

Butter Steak

5 pounds round steak
1/2 teaspoon black pepper
2 cups flour
1/4 pound butter
salt

The steak should be cut about ½ inch thick. Pound the steak with a sprinkling of flour and the pepper, using a mallet or the back of a knife. Prepare a paste of the remaining flour with butter, spread the steak on both sides, and broil. In ranch kitchens a broiler was practically unheard of, and the steak was baked in a very hot oven. This still is a good idea because the butter coating has a way of dripping and smoking unbearably.

No matter how tough the round steak of a range steer might be, the flank would make it seem tender by comparison. Yet most camp cooks tackled Flank Steak, and the men found it delicious when treated as follows.

Score the steaks on both sides, cutting diagonally in opposite angles across the muscle fiber. Paint over with vinegar and lay one on the other for 1 hour. Render the suet in a Dutch oven or large, covered skillet. Pepper the steaks and fry. When brown on both sides, cover with a layer of turnips and onions cut in eighths.

Salt and pepper, cover tightly, and cook at low heat. After ½ hour add the potatoes. As soon as the potatoes are done remove the cover, increase the heat, and serve as soon as the steak has started once more to fry.

FLANK STEAK

5 pounds flank steak
1/4 cup vinegar
1 pound suet
salt and pepper
3 large turnips
3 large onions
2 medium potatoes

19

Build a campfire, using hardwood. Although some hardwoods such as cottonwood give a strong smoke, particularly if still a little green, they impart no lingering taste of turpentine as do the conifers. Quaking aspen was a favorite in the West because it made a fire that was almost smokeless, quite an advantage if one was avoiding Indians, or if he didn't care to attract the interest of some cattle scout or range detective. In all times campers are the object of suspicion, and, law abiding though you may be, it never hurts if they don't even know you're there.

Keep the fire burning briskly from the match onward, adding larger and larger wood, finally trunk and branch pieces as thick through as the arm. Allow it to die and form coals.

Cut willow roasting-sticks about 5 feet long with the small end about the size of the little finger. Cut ribbons of salt pork and dip in boiling water for a few seconds so they will soften and cling when wrapped around the stick. Cut steak in a long spiral starting at the outer edge and ending at the bone. If the steak is ½ inch thick, the ribbons should be about ½ inch wide. Fasten steak, with wire or heavy, wet twine and wrap around the salt pork until you have something that looks like an elongated cattail. A large round steak will weigh a couple of pounds, so it will require two roasting-sticks. Prop the sticks firmly so they will bow over the coals.

TORCH STEAK

round steak, cut thin
salt pork

21

Tend carefully, especially after the heat has penetrated to the salt pork and caused grease to run through because every so often one of the steaks will catch fire. Flames will enhance the flavor, leaving a savory salty flavor behind, but don't make too good a thing of it. Each time a fire breaks out calmly turn the stick; or, the flames persisting, lay your torch steak briefly in the grass.

Cooking meat over an open fire always takes longer than one expects. On a windy night, in fact, the steak never will cook, and a reflector will have to be built to hold in the heat. A board will do, or a lean-to of green poles. A large gold-pan makes the best of all reflectors. Build a place for it among rocks stacked one on the other and tilt it toward the coals, or over the edge of the coals. Some trial and error may be required, but as a rule the fire should blow into the reflector, and it is best to keep the meat in the eddy between the reflector and the fire. If you use a gold-pan, don't leave any grease spatters on it if you want to use it for panning. Grease will form a film on the fine colors and cause them to float right off with the sand.

Stick-Bread or Siwash Biscuit can be baked at the same time as the steak. Make the dough into a ribbon and wrap it around the stick above the meat. If placed below, the grease running over it will turn the crust black with no benefit to the flavor. Meat is one thing and bread is another.

Out on the range, cooks always preferred a calf to a full-grown beef. The meat was tender without aging, and of a size that could be used up and no worry about spoilage. Also, a calf was needed for making a proper Son-of-a-Bitch Stew, more of which later on. Veal steaks and chops were fried, no special recipe, but as many didn't care for the flavor of veal, some doctoring was often deemed advisable. The following Veal Steak was popular.

Cut round steaks ½ inch thick and dredge with flour, sprinkle with pepper but do not salt. Slice bacon and fry until crisp. Remove the bacon and fry the steaks. When they are browned on both sides, pour off any excess bacon grease and add some liquid from the crock where dried fruit has been soaking. If the juice has started to ferment, so much the better. Cover and allow to steam until a gravy forms. Serve the steaks with bacon.

VEAL STEAK

veal round steak
pepper
flour
bacon
juice from dried fruit

STEWS

Choose beef containing a minimum of bone and fat. Cut into cubes about 2 inches across. Dust with flour, pepper, and fry slowly in a Dutch oven, letting it form its own grease. After 15 or 20 minutes add water to almost cover, fit on the lid, and move to a low heat. Allow it to cook for about 3 hours.

Remove the meat, put in another pan to keep warm. Blend the flour with the canned milk and add to the liquid. You should now have about 4 inches of light gravy. Taste for salt. Onions were not always part of the camp cook's larder, but if onions are desired, they can be sliced thin and added at this time. Allow the onions to cook for a few minutes while the dumplings are being mixed. Several favorite dumpling recipes are given later in the book. Whichever recipe is chosen, make the dumpling dough very pasty. When ready, dip a large spoon in the hot gravy, cut a generous portion of the dough, and immerse the spoon. Tap gently on the bottom of the Dutch oven

WARBONNET STEW
ALSO CALLED WAHOO AND ROCKY MOUNTAIN

15 pounds stewing beef
1/2 cup flour
1 tall can milk
salt and pepper
3 or 4 onions
dumplings as made with
   10 cups flour

until the dumpling is released. Repeat, dipping the spoon each time and immersing the dough. When the pot seems full of dumplings, go right ahead, poke the spoon through to the bottom, and keep it up until the dough is all used. Cover and steam slowly for 15 minutes. The dumplings will rise very high and quite likely push up the top of the Dutch oven. You will now have a pot full of dumplings, top to bottom, all gravy disappeared.

Old-time camp cook Charles Baker attributed the name Warbonnet Stew to the bursting spread of dumplings which could be likened to an Indian's headdress, but John Nolan, cook on many roundups, said this was fanciful, that it was merely a favorite recipe of a cook working on the old Warbonnet Ranch in Montana's Little Rockies. Men in the southern ranges called it Rocky Mountain because it was a favorite in the northern mountain regions; Wahoo, apparently, was a cowboy's expression of pure delight. A large helping of stewed beef with a dumpling on top, big as two fists, was as good a dish as a cookwagon ever offered.

Mulligan is an Irish name and Mulligan is an Irish stew, so it is easy to assume it was named for an Irish cook named Mulligan. Not so. When the Irish came West in 1869, unrolling the Union Pacific Railroad behind them, they had a descriptive phrase for a heavy-legged, buxom girl, "Beef by the heels like a Mullingar heifer." Mullingar was a town 50 miles northwest of Dublin famed for its farm market. It was natural that the catch-all stews of a later time, particularly in the western railroad jungles, would be called Mullingar stews because they were likely to contain heel and shank meat, the only lean beef the hoboes could beg from the butcher shops. The earliest printed reference to the stew calls it "Mulliga." Soon it became Mulligan, and is to this day.

Ranch cooks, many of whom doubled as cooks on the railroad work trains, early adopted the Mulligan, and developed personal versions of it. Although the Mulligan varied widely in its contents, it always contained meat, potatoes, and onions, and, generally, canned tomatoes. Along Jim Hill's Great Northern the most famed of Mulligan stews was the one served, more or less gratis, over the bar by James Murphy, saloonkeeper.

Put beef, bones, onions, black pepper, and salt in a large kettle. Murphy used a copper wash boiler. Add cold water to cover the meat. Bring the water slowly to a boil. A grayish scum will rise and

MULLIGAN STEW

20 pounds good, solid beef
 in cubes
20 potatoes
20 onions
2 large soupbones, sawed
1 heaping tablespoon
 whole black pepper
1 gallon tomatoes
water
salt to taste

27

should be skimmed off. Cover and boil very slowly for 3 hours. Add the tomatoes, boil for another ½ hour. Skim off the excess grease. Add the potatoes and set off the stove. If the potatoes are quartered, there will easily be enough heat remaining to cook them through.

Murphy served the stew on large tin plates with 2-inch chunks of hard-crusted, ash-hued bread, which in those times was available from the south-of-Europe railroad section laborers and baked in outdoor brick ovens. The bread was particularly delicious broken and dropped into the stew like ragged croutons.

Select moderately fat stewing beef, remove any large bones, and cut into 2-inch cubes. Put to boil in enough water to cover, add the vinegar, onions, and salt. Cover the pot and cook for about 2 hours, then remove the cover, increase the heat, and boil the liquid away. Use care not to scorch the brown residue. Pepper the meat and fry, turning constantly. Add several handfuls of flour, then water, and stir until a rich brown gravy forms. This is a very hearty dish and a universal favorite among hard-riding men buffeted by the winds on raw days. It is at its best served with baking powder biscuits. Some cooks made an extra generous amount of gravy and baked the biscuits like dumplings on top, while others baked the biscuits separately and broke them in half to form a base over which to ladle the stew.

RICH BEEF STEW

10 pounds beef
1/2 teaspoon ground black pepper
3 or 4 onions
flour
2 tablespoons vinegar
water
1 heaping tablespoon salt

Miners in remote company boarding houses and soldiers at neglected army posts learned to despise corned beef as no other food. They hated beans and salt pork also, but corned beef, put up in tubs, contained saltpeter in its brine pickle, and saltpeter was blamed, rightly or not, for most of the failures of their digestive systems. An old song of the wagon crews that worked their way to California in the years after '49 went:

> Oh, wormy beef and rancid pork
> And bread without the risin'
> They fed us even worse than that
> Good Gawd, but it war pizen.

The "pizen" was generally considered to be saltpeter.

Cooks faced with the necessity of feeding their men on a diet of beans, salt pork, and corned beef, with bread and root vegetables, were likely to give up and just cook in the easiest stew-pot manner. Now and then, however, a cook was equal to the challenge. The following corned beef dinner is excellent:

Soak the corned beef for several hours in cold water and vinegar, then bring it slowly to a boil. Boil only a few minutes, discard the liquid, and put in fresh water. The soaking and parboiling will remove most of the salt, while the vinegar will have a sweetening, tenderizing

CORNED BEEF DINNER

6 pounds corned beef
1 bay leaf
2 heads cabbage
1 teaspoon thyme
6 onions
2 teaspoons allspice
6 potatoes
1/2 cup pork fat
12 carrots
1 can milk
horseradish sauce
1/2 cup vinegar
1/4 teaspoon black pepper

tenderizing effect. Add bay leaf, thyme, and allspice, and boil gently for about 3 hours, until tender. Chop the cabbage and onions, quarter the carrots and potatoes. Put to boil in the pot with the meat. Cook until done. Remove the corned beef and put on a platter with the potatoes and carrots. Add the bacon fat. Make a thickening of flour and canned milk. Cook, stirring until smooth. Serve the onion and cabbage with the resulting gravy in a separate dish. Cut the corned beef into serving pieces. Sprinkle with black pepper and horseradish sauce.

Remember, this was the old-fashioned corned beef. By comparison, today's market corned beef is a delicacy. And don't try preparing canned corned beef in this manner. Canned corned beef makes an excellent camper stew just by boiling a few minutes, thickening a little with flour, and adding dumplings.

The most famed jerky was dried buffalo. Jerky was also made of beef, mountain sheep, antelope, and members of the deer family. It is the lean meat, typically the long muscles, cut in strips lengthwise with the fiber, and hung to dry. In the dry plains the heat of the sun was sufficient. Closer to the sea it was dipped in salt water, and where the climate was excessively damp or cold, it was dried over fires. The higher jerky was hung to dry the better. High up it got more wind and was away from flies. Early ranchers liked to hang their strips of meat for jerky from the platform of a windmill. Indians did not ordinarily concern themselves about flies, and there was little danger of maggots if the drying proceeded fast enough. Jerky hung on rawhide lines for drying resembled clotheslines with a wash consisting wholly of heavy black sox. After being dried, jerky was stored in packages and could be kept for years.

The toughness and quality of jerky depended on its age and the animal it came from. The most resistant jerky came from a bull moose. Moose jerky, cut in wide slabs from low down on the shank, could be used to sole boots of the more rugged sort. It was not highly esteemed. New jerky made from calves, dry cows and does, and from fat mountain sheep could be eaten straight, without cooking, and that was how much of it was consumed by travelers and prospectors who did not want to stop long enough to make a stew.

JERKY STEW

jerky
salt
water
flour

33

Stewing was the only way of cooking it. There was nothing to be gained in roasting dehydrated meat over a fire. The Indians boiled their jerky by lining a hole with rawhide, filling it with water, and dropping in hot stones. The stones were removed as the hole filled, reheated, and dropped back in. It was a steady task, and an unpleasant one. Much has been written about the value an Indian would trade in furs to obtain guns and whisky. The earliest traders found that, after a knife, the most sought article was an iron kettle. After boiling for several hours the jerky became swollen, and eventually broke down into long strings of muscle. The stew was dipped out into cups of one kind or another, those made of alder bark preferred. The meat was eaten with the fingers. One dipped the middle and index fingers to strain out the shreds. When very long they were wrapped around the fingers with a turning and swirling motion in the manner of spaghetti around a fork. The liquid was blown cool before drinking.

Mountain men made dumplings for their stew by forming balls of dampened flour and boiling them, no baking powder or yeast required. A better grade of dumpling was obtained by adding some finely chopped fat. If a dough containing a generous helping of fat is mixed until smooth, if it is then laid on a flat surface and worked by strong strokes of a bowie knife, and if the process is repeated for about 20 minutes, the dough can be cut into squares and boiled to form something like a combined dumpling and noodle. But more of all this later on.

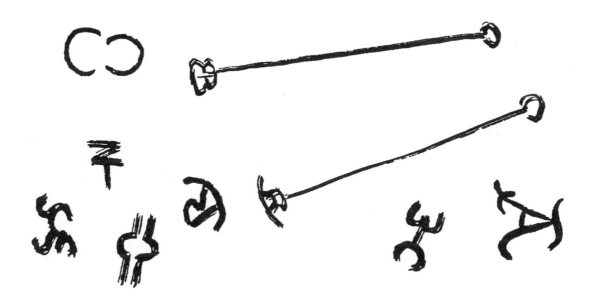

COOKWAGON SPECIALTIES

Like many great results, Son-of-a-Bitch Stew had its origin in necessity. An animal was butchered, and the cook had to prepare something for supper. Even by camp standards the flesh would not be ready for a day. The various organs, however, could be cooked immediately. As there was not enough of any one for the entire crew, the cook combined them all.

Son-of-a-Bitch Stew could be made of beef, but veal was preferred. Veal giblets were tender and had a better flavor. The liver of veal could be added in solid amounts without a resulting bitter taste. Chiefly, veal was preferred because of something called marrowgut. This was the passage connecting the two stomachs of a calf. If the calf had not been too long weaned, it remained full of a cheeselike substance, and this, rather than the organ itself, imparted to the stew its most prized and distinctive flavor.

Assuming you are the cook, you will not do the butchering your-

SON-OF-A-BITCH STEW

Veal heart, tongue, kidneys,
  sweetbreads, marrowgut,
  liver, brains, and suet
flour
salt
pepper
water

37

self, but you will want to be on hand with a bucket when the animal is drawn to make sure none of the useful organs are thrown away. Cut them out, discarding the connective tissue, and put them to soak in cold water to which a handful or two of salt has been added. Trim away what seems to be too tough, especially the large veins and any questionable tubelike passages. Cube the remainder. Take some of the suet from around the kidneys and render in a Dutch oven. Dip the cubes in flour and put to fry, one piece at a time. The heart will require longer cooking and should be put in first. Follow with the tongue. The brains should go in last. It is generally safest to put in only 1 or 2 pounds of the liver. Add salt and pepper, pour in enough water to start the stew to steaming—about 1 inch in the bottom will be enough—cover, and cook slowly for several hours. The liquid should then be almost gone and the stew, each piece of it, nicely coated in brown gravy when served.

Son-of-a-Bitch Stew was more common in the southern cow country than in the North. The author never heard of the stew on his home range, northern Montana, when he was growing up, but there was much talk of something called Son-of-a-Bitch-in-a-Sack. There were in fact two sons-of-bitches-in-a-sack, the one which follows, and a dried fruit pudding described later.

The Scots who came to prairie Canada in large numbers esteemed their Haggis, which was made by cooking the meats listed, and perhaps the lungs and chitterlings as well, with oatmeal, onions, and aromatic herbs inside the stomach of the animal, generally a sheep. The Indians also prepared a Haggis of sorts by filling a buffalo stomach with blood and boiling it gently over a fire, the rennet acting to form a dense, tough, almost black substance which could be sliced like a stiff gelatin when cold. The cowboys' Haggis was made not in the stomach of the butchered animal, but boiled in a clean, white cotton sack.

An ideal sack would be about 24 inches high and 8 inches in diameter. As nothing comes in a sack of that size, you may wish to use a 50-pound flour sack with a fold sewed down the length of it. An easier and more satisfactory way of securing a sack of almost any diameter is by weighting it with a rock. Choose a large pebble from the creek. If slightly flattened by erosion, the average pebble will weigh approximately 1 pound for each inch of its diameter. An 8-pound pebble, therefore, will pull the sack down to a convenient 8-inch diameter. When properly weighted, dip the sack in water. Hang it up and open the throat with a hoop of willow. Dust inside with flour or farina. Dip it again, and if necessary cut a small hole in the bottom to let the water run out. Dust again. Repeat dipping and

SON-OF-A-BITCH-IN-A-SACK I

Veal heart, tongue, kidneys,
   sweetbreads, marrowgut,
   liver, brains, and suet
flour
salt
pepper
water

39

dusting with flour until the inside has built up a thick coat of dough.

Cube the meats as in the preceding recipe. Finely chop the suet. Add suet in amounts of about 1 pound to 6 pounds of meat. Salt and pepper, coat heavily with flour, and spoon into the sack. Take care not to break off the dough coating. When half- or two-thirds full, remove the hoop and tie the top. Set the sack in a large bucket of boiling water. The rock will lift the bottom of the mixture several inches and prevent burning no matter how hot the fire, but the bucket will have to be extra deep. Many cooks brought along special large receptacles for the purpose. Keep boiling 5 or 6 hours. When it is done, lift the sack out and set it down in the creek, in the spring, or the coldest water available. Allow it to set solid. When cold all the way through, strip the sack away. Your Son-of-a-Bitch will then be a rounded, grayish, sausagelike object with the folds of the sack imprinted in it. If it is not too thick through, and if all has gone well, you may, with care, be able to cut perfect round slices. These are particularly delicious fried in bacon fat. When sage has been added to the mixture, Pennsylvanians may tell you it is quite like their native scrapple.

Put all the ingredients in a large pot, nearly cover with cold water, and bring to a brisk boil. Take off the fire for a few minutes, skim, then cover and keep just at the boiling point for about 4 hours. Discard bones, gristle, and fat. Using a potato masher, break down and partially shred the beef so it will mix with the soup as evenly as possible. Pour out in greased loaf pans. When thoroughly chilled, the soup will turn to gelatin so stiff the loaves can be sliced and served on cold dummy, or day-old bread. On hot bread it would quickly revert to soup. Gelatinized stew was called Rainy Day because it was likely to be served on mornings when the weather was too wet for the cook to start a fire. Not all crews had cooks with foresight enough to prepare anything as delicious as Rainy Day when a storm threatened. These poor fellows had to get along on scroungings. Typical scroungings consisted of cold biscuit, bacon grease, and perhaps some soaked dried fruits. Cooks were known for their refractory dispositions. Bad-tempered cooks who turned up with scroungings were likely to run into trouble, but cooks who were famed for a good meal of Rainy Day in emergency would be humored in all excess.

RAINY DAY

14 pounds beef
1/2 cup vinegar
several soupbones
1 tablespoon peppercorns
5 pounds onions
2 tablespoons salt
water

41

MOUNTAIN SAUSAGES, ALSO CALLED PRAIRIE SAUSAGES

young beef chitterlings
bacon
pepper
salt

Mountain Sausages are the small intestines of beef roasted with most of their contents—milky, half-digested food—still in them. Because the main bulk of the day's grazing had progressed from the second stomach to this stage only after the animal was well bedded down for the night, a midnight-butchered calf was considered prime for this particular delicacy.

Without cutting the small intestines, clean them of blood and connecting tissue and put to soak in medium brine. Let them soak until the next day. Remove from the brine and tie with string at 8-inch intervals. Cut into sections close to each tying. This will leave a sausage with one end tied, the other open. Cut bacon into strips. Using slices of bacon like wadding in an old-fashioned muzzleloader, push the filling well down inside each sausage. Don't tie both ends or the sausage is likely to burst. Salt and pepper and roast in a very hot oven. When the sausages are brown on all sides and the bacon grease has fried out enough to sizzle in the pan, serve with hot cornbread or farina muffins.

Boudins, the small intestines of buffalo wrapped around a stick and roasted over a fire, was the supreme delicacy of the mountain men. They were cooked in just that manner, cut into about 2-foot lengths, salted or unsalted. They puffed out and later shrank, often with bursting and hissing, and became alternately crisp and chewy. A little green rose briar or alder bark dropped on the coals imparted a smoke flavor.

BOUDINS

chitterlings

salt

43

ROCKY MOUNTAIN OYSTERS
ALSO CALLED PRAIRIE OYSTERS

calf testicles
farina
suet
salt
pepper
canned milk
water

Rocky Mountain Oysters, often called Prairie Oysters, were the testicles removed from bull calves that might grow into select steer beef. Although much talked about, they were not the delicacy of the common people. Boys in the ranch country heard much of Mountain Oysters and lied about eating them. "Hey, fellows, ever try Mountain Oysters? Yum-yum-yum," etc. But not even the cowboys, for the most part, had ever tasted one. Many of them wouldn't even if they'd had the chance. The Mountain Oyster dinner had much of ritual and much of status about it. As a rule it was only for the bosses and distinguished guests.

Once a year, generally early in the summer, the spring calves were brought in for branding. The only way to accomplish this was to bring in the cows with calves at their sides. The cattle were separated according to ownership, and each outfit had its own branding fire. The fires were kept going for days, consuming whole, dead box elder and cottonwood trees, fed in 6-foot lengths. There might be half a dozen branding irons leaning in the fire so a couple would always be hot—and hot meant glowing black, iron with a ruddiness in it—and the heat traveled up the long iron handles, too, so the men always had folded gunnysacks to guard their hands. The roper, mounted on a methodical, heavy-legged, tireless horse, traveled steadily to the herd and back again, dragging calves which he had caught by the hind legs. At the fire the calf was wrestled down and held, one man to each set of feet; he was branded; the dust settled; the stink of burning hair rose in the air; and he bawled. One man with a jackknife was likely to notch an ear for further identification, and another, if it was a bull calf, took the testicles. These were carried to a protected and shady spot, and dropped into a can half filled with salt water.

The roundup was the great cow country event. The owners came, generally in buggies or wagons, with a favorite riding horse led behind. The brand inspector would be there, a cattle buyer or two, a representative of the railroad or a packing house. Congressman so-and-so might show up, and the ranchers liked to bring important guests from the East. Tents would be pitched, whisky would he served, and there would always be one old man, crippled by rheumatism, who was provided with a rocking chair. They were a very democratic bunch, and were on a first-name basis with every-body, but when the whisky was passed around, the cowboys never got a taste of it. Only, perhaps, the foremen. The owners did some riding, appraised the grass, the stock, saw how many far-off strays had got into the range, guessed at the increase and the chances for their own strays wandering to other roundups; they discussed thieves, the weather, old times, taxes, and the government. There never has been a cattleman from 1868 to this day who didn't think the government was trying to put him out of business, and half the time he's been right. Then it was considered sporting for the biggest owner, who might have arrived with his own Chinese cook, to host a dinner of Mountain Oysters.

Remove the Mountain Oysters from the salt water in which they have been kept; trim off the excess tubing and hard connective tissue. Dip in canned milk and roll in farina. While this is in progress, render leaf suet in a heavy pan. Render a plentiful amount—an inch of very hot grease is not too much. Be sure the oysters are generously covered with farina, then fry. Do not put too many in the pan at one time. At a certain heat they will pop with a spatter of hot grease. Remove them when this happens. Serve immediately, frying more as the feast goes on. They should be eaten just as hot as they can be taken into the mouth, the outside crisp, the inner meat very tender and not, in fact, too unlike a real oyster. Mountain Oysters were often served with hot square Johnnycake, and washed down with good wine. Westerners were not fanciers of dry wines. They preferred a heavy port. Ranching nabobs with real class were known to bring ice in heavy burlap with a supply of Piper Heidsieck.

Pemmican is an Indian sausage. The most famous Pemmican was made by the Indians of the North using elk and deer meat, but fine Pemmican was made of buffalo and, later, the early westerners copying the Indians, of beef.

Spread the serviceberries in the sun to dry. Or use saskatoons—they are the same thing. When shriveled and tough, cut the jerky as fine as possible and pound together. Add the peppercorns and salt, tasting for flavor. Keep pounding until everything is reduced to pulp. Render the suet. Natural casings, the intestines of the animal, will be required for packing. Artificial casings will hold the Pemmican but do not allow it to be properly smoke-cured. The casings should be cut in 2-foot lengths, cleaned, and boiled in salt water. Stretch them. The Indians used a willow-frame stretcher of the sort required for mink skins, or they did the job simply by splitting a branch lengthwise, smoothing it, and expanding it by means of a wedge.

Tie one end of the casing. Hang it like a Christmas stocking. Pack it with the pounded mixture, pausing at intervals to pour in the hot rendered suet. Knead the mixture down until the casing is bulged and shining and all air pockets removed. Tie the top, leaving a loop. Set in brine for a few hours, then hang in a smudge of hardwood. Avoid willow, which smokes too strong, imparting what old-timers called an Indian-moccasin, or a sheep-dip flavor. Alder is good wood

PEMMICAN
OR FRONTIER SUMMER SAUSAGE

20 pounds jerky
5 quarts serviceberries
15 pounds suet
salt as needed
black peppercorns
water

47

for smoking, as is rose briar and apple. Hickory is fine, but it does not grow in the West north of Oklahoma.

Likening smoked Pemmican to an Indian's moccasin in flavor was more than a joke to pioneers, because Indian women sometimes filled moccasins with Pemmican to be taken on journeys, it being a fact that travelers wore out their footwear and became very hungry at the same time. They just got a container of water boiling and dropped in the Pemmican, moccasins and all. In a few minutes the water had become a Pemmican soup, and the moccasins were fished out, hot and slippery, and put on. Drying, they were a perfect fit, shaped to every knob and joint of the foot.

Pemmican may be smoked from 12 hours to 2 days. Hung in a dry, well-ventilated place, properly cured Pemmican will keep for upwards of a year.

Heat bacon grease in a skillet. Add flour little by little, creaming as it turns brown. When the grease has absorbed all the flour it easily can, add water, making a thick gravy. Set on the back of the stove and let the fire die. When the stove is cold, the gravy will have turned to a translucent brown crackling, flaked and curling from the pan. Beat the pan gently to remove. A concentrated nibbling, cowboys liked to carry Squaw Candy in their saddlebags. It is good made into sandwiches of cold biscuit.

SQUAW CANDY
ALSO CALLED SLITHERIX

bacon grease
flour
water

BARBECUES & BROILS

As packers cut steers down the backbone into "sides," the steer will have to be specially handled and hung in one piece. Save the hide, but have the hair removed. When the steer has been properly aged, mount whole on a steel bar or pipe which will serve as a spit. The spit should be at least twice as long as the animal. The steer should be laid on its back and the spit placed down the abdominal cavity. Take time to find the center of balance. If it is mounted so one side is 30 or 40 pounds heavier than the other, controlling it during the turning and roasting will be difficult. Using wet rope or flexible wire, fasten the beef tight and close the abdomen. Rub a mixture of salt, pepper, and lard all over the beef and sew it back inside the hide. Lift the spit to supports on which it is to turn.

Some towns in the early West owned barbecue spits made to specifications by blacksmiths. These had cranks to be turned by one or two men, and were mounted on bearings, generally from discarded

BEEF BARBECUE

whole steer
1/2 pound pepper
2 pounds salt
2 pounds lard

wagon wheels. More often they were put together with things at hand. By one arrangement the spit was hung in loops of log chain slung from above, passed over heavy pulleys, allowing the beef to be raised or lowered as desired. Another thing needed is a sheet-metal hood, the best of which were made with a gable and ventilators, to set over the beef and keep the heat in, or else the barbecuing will take exactly forever. The cookfire can be built on the ground, but long pans for coals, or grates for wood or coal, are better. It is best to put one long fire-pan at one side and one on the other, and a third pan to catch the drippings between. Some of the grease and meat liquor will be bound to fall in the fire, but if too much does, the smoke is unpleasant, and ascending in a continuous stench it will affect the quality of the meat. A bucket of water should be kept at hand to fill the drip pan and extinguish the flames, which will be sure to burst out from time to time where grease saturates the hide.

Now that your steer is properly on the spit and the pans set, go a dozen steps away, put down a metal plate, or some sort of fireproof slab easy to shovel from, and build a fire of hardwood. Have plenty of fuel on hand. As much as a cord of wood may be required if your steer is a large one. Hickory, birch, ash, box elder, and apple wood were favored at one place or another. Excellent results were obtained from anthracite coal, which was available in western towns, shipped in for specialized use. When coals are formed, move them a shovelful at a time to the fire-pans. Keep the heat rising without interruption. The hood should always be hot enough to sizzle when tested with the moistened finger.

Barbecuing a beef takes all night and well into the next day. The fire will require constant attention. When the drippings collect, they should be taken up with a brush, or dipped with a tin cup, and used to baste the meat. You will find it necessary to fasten the brush and cup to sawed-off broomsticks. A long, sharpened pole should also be on hand to turn the meat. Even if the spit is equipped with a crank, the heavy beef will frequently jam it, or get slightly off center. The pole can be used as a lever to shift the weight or turn the spit around. No hurry. One complete revolution in 1 hour will be enough.

When the beef approaches the eating stage, certain signs will appear. The meat will pull back from the bones, particularly the shanks. The hide will shrivel, curl back, and become hard as sheet metal. The backbone will bow, and the legs will stand stiffly out. To test the meat make a deep cut in the sirloin. The middle of the loin should be rare. As soon as the loin and deep round become steaming rare most of the beef is well-done. Old-time masters of the barbecue never heard of a meat thermometer, but here is something that served the purpose. Sharpen a spike—it should be a large one, thick

through as a lead pencil—and push it deeply into the loin. Allow it to remain for several minutes. Withdraw it and clamp it against the inside of your wrist. If the heat forces you to grit your teeth to maintain pressure, the meat is done.

Take the fire away. Remove the hide. Make sure the beef is placed correctly, with the back down. Make a table of planks on sawhorses and lower the spit from its supports. Remove the spit and cut the beef in half down the spine using a sharp cleaver. Cut into front and hindquarters, remove the shanks. Carve, starting with the lower round and the prime rib. In this way the front quarter will progress from the highly desirable prime rib, or shortcut, to the shoulder and neck, while the hind will move from shank round to T-bone, making the last in line equal to the first.

Mix all the ingredients except the stale beer, then add the beer until a mixture is obtained which is thin enough to drip from a brush, but not so thin as to refuse the olive oil when it is stirred. Apply this sauce alternately with the meat drippings.

Slice round steak very thin, then cut into shoestrings. With a very sharp knife and a good cutting board you will be able to slice strips 1/8 inch in cross section. Form into patties. Dip in olive oil and then in flour. Sprinkle with Worcestershire sauce and pepper. Broil over hardwood coals. The lean meat will drip far less than hamburger, while the olive oil will impart a subtly delicious flavor. Salt when finished. Shoestring Steaks are best served a trifle rare.

BARBECUE SAUCE

1 cup blackstrap molasses
1/2 cup black pepper
1 cup vinegar
1 pound salt
stale beer as needed
1 quart olive oil

SHOESTRING STEAK BARBECUE

4 pounds round steak
1 tablespoon Worcestershire sauce
1/2 cup olive oil
1/2 cup flour
pepper
salt

Oven-Barbecued Ribs

10 pounds (about) mutton, deer,
    mountain sheep, or elk ribs
1/2 cup sorghum
1/2 teaspoon dry mustard
1/2 cup vinegar
1/2 teaspoon pepper
1 teaspoon paprika
2 teaspoons salt

Mix the sorghum, mustard, vinegar, pepper, paprika, and salt. Using a brush, coat the ribs. Place in a very hot oven with a pan of water to catch the drippings. Turn from time to time and spread with more of the sauce. Cook until the edges show crisp and the coating is brown.

As soon as the Central Pacific was completed to its junction with the Union Pacific in Promontory Point, Utah, the Chinese who had been brought in by the thousands to build grade and drive steel found themselves cut loose in a strange mountain environment. In large gangs they walked, sometimes 500 miles, living off the country, eating berries, beetles, and frogs, until they reached some place where a living could be earned. Many of them ended in the placer-mining camps. Prevented from staking claims, they camped on the tailing-heaps and panned for the minute gold particles, or "colors," the white men had let escape. They also went into business. Most of the laundries were Chinese, as were the opium dens; Chinese doctors treated miners' ills by means of diet, herbs, and the horoscope; and quite a number went into the restaurant business. All over the West, in mining, lumber, and cattle towns, the best food was likely to be prepared by the Chinese. Noodles, chop suey, and foong gai might be midnight specialties, but the average miner and timber-stiff favored the standard roasts, chops, stews, and pies. The Chinese, while meeting the demand, still never quite subverted their long culinary tradition. Pork in particular tasted different in a Chinese restaurant than it did elsewhere, and at its best was very good indeed.

Simmer dried fruits—peaches, pears, apricots, apples, any or a mixture—with double their weight of water, and ginger. Set aside.

CHINESE PORK ROAST

pork shoulder
1 teaspoon ginger
1/2 teaspoon salt
1 pound dried fruit
1 quart water
cornstarch
pepper to taste

57

Take the bone from a pork shoulder, opening it so it lies in one piece. Soak for ½ hour in liquor from the dried fruit. Salt and pepper, roll back to its original shape, fasten with skewers, and bake in a hot oven, without cover, until done. Remove, add cornstarch to the pan to thicken, brown, pour in water and a tablespoon or so of the fruit liquor, and make a thin gravy. Pour over the meat after slicing.

Boil the dried fruits with ginger as in the preceding recipe. Bone two pork shoulders and soak them $\frac{1}{2}$ hour in the warm liquor. Mix the stuffing, adding enough water to soak the bread, but do not destroy its life by squeezing it out. Lay the stuffing on one opened shoulder and place the other over it. Skewer together, but do not roll. Steam for $\frac{1}{2}$ hour and then brown. Two boned roasts laid together will cook more quickly than one roast with the bone still in. The Chinese, to preserve the flavor of their pork, served many a roast on the rare, pink, and succulent side, no doubt making business for the herbalist down the street. Pork should be cooked but not over-cooked. It's quite a problem.

Serve your stuffed pork with gravy made in the pan with cornstarch, water, and a few drops of soy.

STUFFED CHINESE PORK ROAST

2 pork shoulders
1 apple
3/4 teaspoon salt
1 stalk celery
1 pound dried fruit
1 powdered sage leaf
1 quart water
1/4 teaspoon thyme
1 teaspoon ginger
1/2 teaspoon salt
2 slices dry bread
cornstarch
soy sauce
1 onion, optional

QUICK FIXINGS

Oh, I like Jim Hill,
He's a good friend of mine,
And that's why I'm farming
By Jim Hill's main line.

When the homesteaders came West to take up 160 acres of land along Jim Hill's Great Northern Railway, they planted spring wheat which turned out to be the best bread-making wheat in the world, turnips which grew to magnificent size and quality in the new-turned sod, and potatoes which were often too small to be considered a commercial product, but were of an excellence beyond compare. They did not have a nutlike flavor, they had a potato flavor, but grop-ing for words such as *nutlike* is the only thing that comes to mind. Their flavor was marvelous. Also, not growing large like the irrigated varieties, they had small starch cells which allowed them to be boiled

JIM HILL T-BONE

cold boiled potatoes
onions
stale sourdough
eggs
bread
butter
water

61

overdone without turning into a mush. Homesteaders were lucky to have such good potatoes because in dry years potatoes were likely to form the chief bulk of their diet. A standard way of serving potatoes was to parboil them underdone, and fry them, when cold, with onions and dampened bread, in butter. If two or three fried eggs were then blanketed over the top of each serving, one had the standard dryland farmer's dinner, so universally served it was referred to as the Jim Hill T-Bone.

Put medium- or small-size unpeeled potatoes in cold water, bring to a boil, then set off the stove. When cool they will be cooked through, but solid, and the best texture for either frying or salad making. Half an hour before mealtime, melt several tablespoons of butter in a heavy skillet. If you happen to live in one of the communities where farm butter is still available, you will discover that its strong, sour-milk flavor adds considerably to the final result. While the butter is still foaming, slice in an onion, cover, and allow to fry. Peel the potatoes and cut into wedges about the size of Brazil nuts. Fry, stirring gently and adding butter if needed. When the onions are done and the pieces of potato have about one browned side each, soak the stale bread in water, wring out, crumble in pan, stir, and add more butter if needed. Cover lightly and set aside. Fry eggs in butter sunnyside up or over-easy as desired. Over-easy means you flop the eggs over, but carefully, so as not to break the yolks, then rescue before the yolks are solid through. Place a large scoop of fried potatoes on each plate. Carefully, so as not to break the yolks, lay the desired number of eggs on top. Black pepper may be added to the potatoes, but it is customary for each to pepper his eggs to taste. The butter may contain sufficient salt without addition. Some people ate their potatoes and eggs separately, but they risked being thought high-toned and putting on airs. The eggs were properly served right on top where, with a few swift knife cuts, the yolks would be set free to seep downward through the potatoes, the fried bread, the onions, and the strong butter. Delicious.

63

BACHELOR'S DINNER

canned cream-style corn
cold bread or biscuits
canned milk
bacon grease

Many of those who came West to take free land were single men. For them Jim Hill T-Bone was out of the question. They raised no chickens, milked no cows, churned no butter. Coming home to their lonely shacks, they were lucky to find cold biscuits, solidified bacon grease with brown drippings in the bottom, and some canned goods. For them the most standard of hot meals consisted of canned corn and biscuits.

Heat canned corn and canned milk in a skillet until bubbling. Add crumbled bread or biscuit until a desirable consistency is attained. Cut cold biscuits in half, spread with bacon grease, heat grease side up on top of stove. When the grease disappears and the biscuits are hot, transfer to a plate and pour the corn over them.

The bachelor homesteader frequently supplemented this with a can of tomatoes. Few dry land claims had a water supply. Wells were expensive. Water was hauled or caught in a cistern, and either way it was likely to develop a stale, sulfury taste. The juice from a can of tomatoes was an excellent thirst quencher, while the solid fruit, with sugar, was dessert. He was likely to take both directly from the can and dispose of the latter, when empty, simply by walking to the door and throwing it as far as possible. Or on a fine day he probably ate outside, standing where the wind blew, listening to the meadowlarks, and taking in the view, which was immense. His plate, a tin one, was polished clean with sagebrush, leaving it smelling better than soap. The frying pan, allowed to remain on the stove with the remnants of corn and milk in it, had by the time his meal was finished dried down to a state where no sagebrush would touch it. This did not worry the bachelor homesteader. He left it right there on the stove where still a few coals were glowing, knowing that by night everything would be dry to crackling and would flake out clean if he just took the pan outside and beat it, clang-clang, on the side of the house.

All in all, bachelors didn't have it too hard. They regarded farm life as camping out, and spent much time going back and forth to town, which might be only 20 or 30 miles away. As it was almost impossible to heat a tarpaper-covered, rough-board shack in the winter, even when it was banked with dirt to the window sills, most bachelors hoboed to Washington and got jobs in the woods, returning with a stake sufficient to put in a crop the next spring. They led a life short on comforts but long on freedom.

BUTTE PASTIE

3 pounds beefsteak
2 teaspoons salt
3 onions
1/4 teaspoon pepper
5 medium-size potatoes
1/2 cup butter,
  or 1/2 cup chopped salt pork
flour
pie dough
lard

Cut the steak and potatoes into 1/2-inch cubes, chop the onions, mix, add salt and pepper, and put in a warming oven. Make a dough such as you might use for pies, except add a trifle more than the usual amount of water. The dough derived from 6 cups of flour should be sufficient. Roll out, cut into circles using the outside of a small pie tin for the pattern. Dip about 2 cups of the mixture onto the center of each. Sift a little flour over the filling and dot with butter. (Or instead of butter you may add 1/2 cup of chopped salt pork to the mixture.) Wet the edges and pinch together. Some cooks use canned milk. If so, go easy because milk will glue the pastie fast to the pan when baking. Use a flat, greased pan and bake about an hour in a hot oven. As no two cooks put the same amount of filling in their pasties or fold them to the same thickness, the baking time will vary. To test, cut a small hole and remove a cube of potato. It should be well-done and full of meat flavor.

Pasties are delicious hot or cold. In Butte they were great favorites, going into the miner's lunch to be eaten underground. One or two formed a complete meal, and could be eaten without knife or fork—no waste, no muss. The Cornish "Cousin Jacks" who came West to work in the mines brought the pasties with them, and the Irish, learning what boardinghouses did with stew, adopted them also. Mining camp stew was dumped hot into the dinner pails; it solidified and had to be dug out and eaten cold. A pastie had cold stew beat a mile. Small fruit pies could be made in the same manner, carried and eaten without waste, without implements. A couple of pasties and a pie certainly combined a lot of fuel, but there weren't many fat miners, not in the old hand-steel and doublejack days anyhow.

FORT LINCOLN

5 pounds cold roast
1 can milk
6 large potatoes
1 cup flour
1 pound salt pork
water as needed
salt and pepper
bacon grease

Traditionally, the cold roast was pork, but lamb, veal, beef, or venison will work just as well.

Peel the potatoes and put them on to boil. After about 10 minutes, fry the salt pork, sliced medium thin, until crisp. Store in a warmer. Add flour to the hot grease, creaming against the bottom of the pan until uniform and brown. Add water and make a gravy. Add the canned milk. Keep stirring. When smooth and fairly thin in consistency, add the roast cut into cubes. Keep warm and run the potatoes through a ricer. If preferred, they may be mashed and whipped. Make a circle of potatoes on a large platter, pour the meat and gravy inside. Place the crisp salt pork here and there on the potatoes.

TROUT & LESSER FISH

This is the famed oven-fried trout of the old McDonald Lake log hotel of the 1890s.

An ideal trout for oven-frying is fresh and cold from a mountain stream, and about 12 inches in length. Dress, leaving the head and tail intact. Heat the oven to 450 or 500 degrees. For half a dozen trout of the above length, melt 1 pound of butter in a pan. If you can find ranch butter, use it. It will contain more sour milk and brown more deeply. The pan should fit the number of trout. For half a dozen 12-inch trout and 1 pound of butter, an old-fashioned, black, sheet-metal, three-loaf bread pan will prove about right.

Make a mixture of fine-rolled bread crumbs and flour. Either alone will do, but a mixture will coat better and not flake off during the cooking. Remove the trout from the wet cold where they have been kept, let the excess water drip off, and roll in the floured crumbs. Dry your hands before touching the coated trout or else your fingers will

OVEN-FRIED TROUT

mountain trout
bread crumbs
flour
butter

come off breaded and part of the trout not. Lay each coated trout on a dry towel.

Wait until the butter has melted, foamed, settled, and started to "cluck." Now, carefully holding each trout by its jaw, slide it tail first into the smoking-hot butter. Get your hand back quickly because the sudden cold and inner moisture is likely to cause a miniature explosion of oil droplets. When all the trout are in, they should fill the pan so the butter rises and almost covers them. Baking in a properly hot oven will not take long. Keep watch, and as soon as the trout look golden-brown test the flesh with a long fork. When one tine sinks in easily and with slight pressure breaks some of the white or pinkish flesh free of the backbone, remove the pan. Lift all the trout at once, or several at a time, by means of spatulas. Lifting them singly will certainly cause some of them to break up. If cooked correctly, they will be medium-brown, will hold together when served, but will be tender enough so the backbones can be removed with heads and tails attached, the flesh left all but boneless. A sprinkle of salt may be desired, but chances are there will be enough salt in the butter.

Early-day tourists who visited the small mountain hotels went away telling about the marvelous trout, and oven-fried was how they got them. They were a hardy breed, those early sightseers, compared with today's trailer folk. Alighting from the Northern Pacific, they traveled by stagecoach, which was likely to be little but an omnibus wagon, to see the wonders of Yellowstone National Park, the famed Flathead Lake, and the everlasting glaciers of the Lewis Range. The least of these journeys required at least a week. Seeing the glaciers in the days before the Great Northern was built was truly an adventure. One had to alight from his Northern Pacific Pullman Palace car at Ravalli, then known as Second Crossing, west of Missoula, and take the old Hell Gate and St. Ignatius wagon road to Polson Bay on Flathead Lake. This was a long day's journey, and generally it required camping along the way. From Polson a steam ferry was available to Demersville at the northern end of the lake. Another two-day journey by wagon put the travelers within walking distance of McDonald Lake. Walk they did, using an ancient Indian path through the timber. When the Great Northern reached Belton, a road was cleared, a steamboat assembled, and a log hotel built near the head of the lake. It was the first accommodation within what was later set aside as Glacier National Park. From the hotel, anyone who truly wished to see the Sperry, Blackfoot, or Harrison glaciers had yet a rugged climb and perhaps a night in the open, hotel saddle horses being at that time an undreamed-of luxury. A trip to McDonald and back required three weeks, minimum, but few complained. Memory of the trip through a wilderness of unblemished purity and grandeur was treasured after

the humps, jolts, mosquitoes, and deluge were long forgotten.

The early hotel at McDonald, like most of the others of the region, specialized in such things as mountain trout, black bear roasts, and venison chops. Butter, eggs, and vegetables came from the Flathead Valley, but for entrees it was largely no-catch, no-eat. Its culinary fame was based on necessity. Making a specialty of trout, it offered the chief thing it had. Its superb oven-fry, famed among pioneering guests, was likewise a matter of no-choice. Food was served American plan, and the oven of an old-fashioned wood range provided the only means of getting a sufficient quantity to the table all crackling hot and delicious at the same instant.

This is a campfire dish, often the quickest and simplest meal that can be prepared, but dudes, introduced to Boiled Trout by their wilderness guides, returned home proclaiming it the best fish in their memory. Later many of them tried to prepare market trout in the same manner and were disappointed. It was then assumed that their original judgment was due to hunger and the open air. Hunger and the open air help, but the guide probably served trout taken from the purest and coldest water. A trout caught in warmer water, or when the streams are low and weedy, might receive fewer accolades. By no method is the delicate flavor of the fish—or its musty, low-water taste—so preserved. Just as a rough rule, no trout should be boiled that comes from water which cannot be safely and joyfully drunk. Some trout purists insist if they can't drink the water they don't want the trout that comes from it, boiled, fried, or cooked by any other method—a principle that sends them tramping beyond the last road, far up the rocky canyons.

The best size for boiling is about 14 inches. Dress, leaving the head and tail on. Have a large pot of water boiling. No salt. Just drop the fish in the boiling water. With a pointed willow test the shoulder of the fish to see how things are progressing. The time required will vary with the altitude. Some trout lakes are very high, reducing the boiling point of water to under 190 degrees. When the trout is done but not overdone, lift it from the water. This is a very sophisticated point, and requires

BOILED TROUT

trout
boiling water
butter

experience. Whenever a bit of the flesh breaks off in the testing, it is time. Laid flat it should break open along the back, allowing the bones, from head to tail, and with head and tail attached, to be removed in one piece. With bones removed and the flesh laid open, steaming in the cold mountain air, pour melted butter liberally. No further salting will be needed. No pepper, please.

PAN-FRIED TROUT

trout
butter
flour or bread crumbs
salt

Clean the trout without removing heads, tails, or fins. Keep them damp and cold in wrappings of grass or water weeds until just before cooking. Salt inside. Roll in flour or in finely powdered bread crumbs. Some cooks use cornmeal, but this is better for catfish, sturgeon, and similar river fish. Melt butter generously in a heavy skillet. Lard or vegetable oil may be used, but if so add a lump of butter for flavor. Keep the skillet at a medium, uniform heat for about 5 minutes. Put the trout in without crowding. After about ½ minute, lift each in turn so fresh butter can flow beneath and prevent scorching. Cover lightly, not enough to steam but enough to enclose some of the heat. Turn, leave the cover off, add butter if needed, and serve as soon as the second side is brown and the flesh tender. Pan-size trout do not take long to cook, but don't worry, a good trout fried in butter is delicious whether fried little, medium, or much.

Baked River Fish

whole fish, 4 to 8 pounds
1 onion
cracker crumbs
1 carrot
1/4 pound salt pork
1 teaspoon vinegar
1 cup canned milk
1 tablespoon sugar
1 cup water
salt and pepper
capers, sweet pickles optional

The fish can be a channel cat, a small sturgeon, a carp from good water, or a trout—Dolly Varden, Loch Laven, or a big, river-going rainbow. Dress, removing head and tail. Skin fish or scale it, depending on the species. Even trout which are not customarily scaled often require a little work when they're in the large size. Heat a roaster in a hot oven, about 400 degrees, and fry salt pork slices until crisp. Remove the pork, dredge the fish inside and out in cracker crumbs, and start it sizzling in the grease. Add the canned milk, water, sliced onion, and quartered carrot. Cover, cut down the heat, and cook until the fish, onion, and carrot are well-done. Salt and pepper to taste. Remove the fish carefully to prevent breaking it. Garnish with the carrots, onion, and crisp salt pork. A quantity of milk thickened by cracker crumbs will remain in the pan. To this add the vinegar and sugar, and more if taste requires. A few capers will lend a spicy interest. Some cooks forego sugar, vinegar, and capers and add chopped sweet pickles. Blend until smooth and serve as a sauce.

Soak the codfish in cold water. When soft, shred and put back in fresh cold water. Peel potatoes, quarter, and boil. When the potatoes are almost done, drain the water from the codfish and add to the potatoes. Boil together. After 4 or 5 minutes drain, mash the potatoes and codfish into a smooth puree, add the bacon fat, and beat hard using a wooden spoon. Add the canned milk a little at a time and keep beating. When smooth, pour into a baking dish, pepper, sprinkle with cornmeal, and bake until lightly brown.

CODFISH DINNER

2 pounds salt codfish
1 small can milk
4 medium potatoes
1/2 cup bacon fat
pepper
cornmeal

Curtis Wells
Wyo. Terr.
Oct 3, 1883

Dear Friend:

Hope you are all
well. I've had the
most terrible journey
(four)
4 days by wagon
and nothing but beans
sowbelly (salt) and alkali
coffee. also most godforsaken
country — two mules
sick from what Old
"Blow" claimed to
be la grippe equine
style but which in my
opinion is nothing more nor

over

BEANS

Although a staple of diet, the bean was not highly regarded by those who took their fare at the cookwagon. Granted some cooks were very good with baked beans; still the term "sowbelly and bean outfit" was one of derision. Cowboys agreed that the farther north they traveled the better, in general, was the grub, and the fewer the beans. Also, when the northern outfits, those located from Wyoming to Alberta, did load heavily on beans, they purchased the more costly white varieties. The cheap, rough-cooking blackeye, pinto, and dark beans were favored by the owners, if not the cooks and cowboys, of outfits down toward the Rio Grande. Firehole Beans was given its name by cowboys up in the northern range when the cook prepared the dark ones more or less in the Boston-baked manner. "Firehole" in this case was not related to pit roasting, although this method was sometimes used, but was a corruption of frijoles, the name for beans in Spanish.

FIREHOLE BEANS

1 quart black beans
1/2 pound salt pork
3 quarts water
2/3 cup blackstrap molasses
1 rounded tablespoon salt
1 teaspoon dry mustard
1 can tomatoes

Using a galvanized pail, soak the beans overnight. Pour off the top water and with it any floaters, twigs, etc. Swirl the beans for a time. This will allow any rocks to go to the bottom just like nuggets in a miner's pan. Lift the beans using the fingers of the two hands as a strainer. Transfer to a heavy iron pot, or Dutch oven, equipped with a well-fitting lid. Add salt and cold water. Bring slowly to a boil and keep boiling for 3 hours, adding water if the level drops beyond what appears to be a safe point. Slice the salt pork into inch-wide strips and cut crosswise, forming squares of fat attached to rind. Add the pork, molasses, mustard, and tomatoes. Cover and bake. If the cooking is done on a campfire, half a shovelful of coals should be kept on the lid. Some outdoor cooks dug a hole in the middle of the fire and set the Dutch oven about half the way down in it, but it had to be an old fire, one which had burned in the same spot for a day or so to make certain its heat had penetrated to a sufficient depth. Bake all day or all night, lifting the cover only to make certain there is a small amount of liquid on top.

Soak the beans overnight, skim off floaters, and pan for stones. It is a popular belief that stones are added intentionally to increase the weight, but for the most part they are picked up from the low stalks in harvesting. Saw the ham bone in half. Push the two parts down among the beans, add water, and boil slowly for about 3 hours. Remove the bone and add the salt, green tomatoes, onions, and peppers, chopped fine. Cover and bake at a low heat for several hours, adding water as needed. If a quart of water is added and allowed to bubble for an hour or so, it can be taken off and served as a very superior soup.

FIREHOLE BEANS II

1 quart pinto beans
3 onions
3 quarts water
2 red chili peppers
1 ham bone
6 green tomatoes
1 tablespoon salt

HOPPING JOHN

1 quart blackeye beans
3/4 quart rice
2 ham hocks
1 dried hot pepper
I tablespoon salt
water

Hopping John was not named for its inventor, which one might imagine to be a spirited fellow named Hopping John. Blackeye beans, or cowpeas, got the name because they grew so fast they seemed to hop right out of the ground. One finds early references to "fields of hopping John," but the term is now applied to a stewed mixture of beans, peppers, and rice. The following standard southern recipe came up the trail with the Texas camp cooks:

Pour the blackeye beans (cowpeas) into boiling water and immediately set aside to cool. Boil the ham hocks for 2 hours. Drain the beans and add them to the ham hocks. Simmer for about 1 hour, or until the beans are tender. Add the rice and crushed red pepper. Be sure there is sufficient liquid because rice requires three to four times its bulk. When the rice is done, remove the ham hocks, leaving lean meat that can be scraped off and served.

An excellent Hopping John can also be made by substituting 1 pound of bacon or salt pork for the ham hocks; by using Tabasco, peppercorns, and chili powder in manageable proportions instead of the dried red pepper; and by adding a can of tomatoes. There is a magic quality to a combination of tomatoes and butter, and when tomatoes are used, butter may be substituted for the fat meat with improved results. In fact, the only unfortunate thing about any of these recipes is the Hopping John bean itself. The cowpea has honestly earned its reputation as a lowly vegetable.

This was the standard baked beans of the northern ranges.

Soak the beans several hours in cold water, throw aside any floaters, pan out any pebbles, and put the beans to boil in salted water. After about 2 hours cut the salt pork into cubes, leaving the rind on, and bake in a heavy iron pot, tightly covered. No molasses, mustard, or catsup. Serve with plenty of broth, heavy with oil and concentrated bean liquor.

Sheepherder cooking was esteemed in the West to be only one step ahead of "squaw cooking," which was considered to be the worst there was; but Sheepherder Beans was the best. In some regions they went by the name of Bachelor-Baked Beans, or Homestead Beans. In all cases the preparation was the same—good, old-fashioned northern baked beans with an excess of salt pork.

Soak the beans overnight, sort, and put to boil in a heavy pot with water and salt. Cut salt pork in slices and drop one after another into the boiling liquid. Continue to boil slowly until done.

This was, of course, not baked beans, but boiled beans. With the equipment at hand the sheepherder couldn't have baked anything even if he'd wanted to. He lived in a canvas-topped wagon equipped with a stove just large enough to heat the wagon during chilly weather

NORTHERN BAKED BEANS

1 quart navy or great
   northern beans
1 pound salt pork
3 quarts water
1 tablespoon salt

SHEEPHERDER BEANS
ALSO CALLED BACHELOR-BAKED BEANS AND HOMESTEAD BEANS

1 quart great northern beans
2 pounds salt pork
1 tablespoon salt
3 quarts water

85

and to cook one dish at a time. If this was a kettle of beans, the sheep-herder merely let it stand until the next time the fire was built. He might just as willingly have eaten cold beans, and during chilly weather he often did, but in the summer he boiled his beans at least once a day, and preferably twice, to protect them against souring. In the winter when the thermometer went down to 40 below zero, nobody tried to live in a canvas-topped wagon, but Sheepherder Beans remained the standard emergency fare in hundreds of lonely cabins and line shacks. Beans cooked with an excess of salt pork never froze hard. They could be dug like tough putty from the pot and melted in the mouth of the starving, or if a man had more time, they could be thawed, made into a soup, or they could be fried. Fried beans are delicious.

FRIED BEANS

Sheepherder Beans
bacon fat
flour

Slice frozen beans—0 degrees or colder—3/4 inch thick. Dip in flour and fry in bacon grease in a very hot skillet. If left in too long, they will melt and become just plain hot beans. Turn as quickly as the flour browns. Serve while still ice cold in the middle.

Sportsmen on pack trips to remote, timberline plateaus have been known to return with tales of privation from uncooked food. The beans were hard, the coffee weak, and nothing came from the stewpot as expected. The problem was altitude. At sea level boiling water exerts a cooking heat of 212 degrees. At 4,000 feet, the average of cow country, it drops to about 204. Bakers of fine cakes may have to adjust the amount of baking powder used—they need less of it—but 204 degrees is still plenty for the stewpot. Beyond a mile, where the heat drops to 202 degrees, boiling times start to lengthen. At 12,000 feet water has a heat of only about 189½ degrees.

As a general rule one should add 10 percent cooking time for each 1,000-foot climb. This works well enough up to around 6,000 feet. At the very high altitudes—around 12,000 feet—it fails because boiling heat isn't enough to cook, say, a pot of beans, even if boiled all week.

The problem of cooking at 12,000-foot altitudes was not often encountered by camp cooks and ranchers, but in southwestern Colorado the mining camps lie around that level, and on the Wyoming-Montana border, hard beside Yellowstone Park, trout fishermen pack in to the lakes of the Beartooth Plateau more than 2 miles high. Some form of pressure-cooking has long been used by the permanent residents of the high altitudes, while campers rely on frying and broiling.

MOUNTAINTOP BEANS
OR BEANS SALTY

1 quart great northern beans
3/4 cup light molasses
1 cup lard
2 quarts water
1 pound salt

Altitude above Sea Level	Boiling Point
0	212
510	211
1,020	210
1,545	209
2,050	208
3,085	206
4,130	204
5,185	202
6,250	200
8,950	195
11,720	190

Things can be boiled, however, if the boiling point is raised by the addition of salt in large quantities.

For beans, dissolve the salt in 2 quarts of water. Boil the beans until they are about the texture of raw peanuts. Pour off the salt water, boil in plain water, pour this off, add 2 cups of water, lard, and molasses. Cover tightly as possible and bake. The molasses, like the salt, will raise the boiling point and promote cooking.

Beans and Brisket

6 pounds beef brisket
2 pounds onions
3 cups navy beans
1 bay leaf
1/2 pound salt pork
1/2 teaspoon peppercorns
1 teaspoon smoke salt
1 gallon water

Soak the beans overnight, drain, and put in the water to boil with the salt pork. Keep just barely bubbling. Cut the brisket into slices and fry in Dutch oven, stirring and turning over continually until sufficient grease has been rendered to guard against burnings. When the pieces are brown on all sides, add the onions, fry for a while, then pour in enough water to cover, add bay leaf and peppercorns, cover, and cook slowly. After about 2 hours remove the brisket and save the liquid. Lay slices of brisket to cover the bottom of the Dutch oven. Next add a layer of sliced onions; follow with a layer of beans, then more brisket, onions, and beans; sprinkle the smoke salt on top. Pour the bean liquor and beef liquor over all, cover, and bake slowly for 2 more hours.

Smoke salt is a fairly recent development. Some early kitchens, however, used a homemade "Indian smoke" for flavoring. According to legend, this was the bottled essence derived from long boiling of Indian moccasins whose strong tepee-smoke odor lasted as long as the leather. Actually, it came from the prolonged smoking of the hocks of beef, pork, or deer. Hocks, being thick with skin, fat, gristle, and marrow, are able to absorb heavy loads of smoke tars, and were much used for their flavor.

SOUPS, CHOWDERS & VEGETABLES

Peel and quarter the potatoes and turnips, cut the onions thin, and boil all together in moderately salted water until tender. Discard the water. Mash. Add 3 cups of boiling water. Cook at low heat, covered. Fry bacon until crisp. Put the slices away where they will keep warm and add the bacon grease to the soup. Make a paste of flour and canned milk, add slowly, stirring. Keep stirring until perfectly smooth, adding more water if required for correct consistency. Salt and pepper to taste. Crumble the bacon and sprinkle over the top just before serving.

DIGGER SOUP

4 potatoes
2 turnips
2 onions
1/2 pound bacon
1 small can milk
1/4 cup flour
salt, black pepper
4 tablespoons bacon grease
salted water

Potato Soup

3 dozen wild prairie onions
1 small can milk
3 potatoes
4 tablespoons butter
salt and pepper
1 tablespoon flour

Parched Corn Dinner

1 1/2 cups parched corn
1/4 pound salt pork, cubed
2 large potatoes
2 slices dry bread
1 tall can milk
salt and pepper
1 small onion, sliced
1 quart water

Make the onions into a bunch, cut off the roots and approximately the top third, chop the remainder, and fry in butter. Cube the potatoes, add water, and boil until they have become rounded. When the potatoes start giving body to the liquid, mix the milk and flour to form a thin paste and add slowly, stirring.

Put on water to boil. Add the onions and salt pork. Sift in the parched corn, stirring all the while, then simmer under a cover. When the corn starts to thicken but does not yet seem to be quite done, put the potatoes on to boil in a separate pan. Keep close watch of the potatoes, and when they are on the hard side of being done, put them in cold water, cut into 1/2-inch cubes, and add to the corn chowder. Now add the can of milk. Salt and pepper to taste. Simmer. If timed correctly, the corn will be done, and the potatoes, while done, will be firm rather than cooked into a mush. Heavily butter the bread and toast on a hot griddle. The toasting will allow the bread to be cut, hot, into cubes. Serve the chowder with the toast cubes floating on top as croutons.

Canned cream-style corn may be substituted for the parched corn. Parched corn is green corn shaved from the ears and dried in the sun. As recently as thirty years ago grocery stores stocked parched corn in 5-pound cloth bags. Perhaps it is still available in some regions or at wilderness outfitters who make a specialty of dehydrated foods. To parch your own: choose fresh green corn, shuck, remove silks, and dip the ears in boiling, salted water. Shave off the kernels, getting as little of the cob as possible. Most of the parched corn had lots of the cob, giving it, when cooked, a coarse texture, as if sawdust had been added, but it doesn't have to be that way. Sprinkle the kernels on cheesecloth pulled tight over a frame, and dry in the sun. When perfectly flaky, press flat with a rolling pin and pack in cloth sacks. Hang in a well-ventilated place. The pioneers hung it by wires from rafters, outwitting the field mice and pack rats that moved inside with winter.

Roast Green Corn

green corn
butter
water

When the old-timers called them "roasting ears," they weren't fooling. They picked the corn very young, generally in the blister stage, and roasted it in the oven, or in the hot ashes. Theirs was the common field corn. Later, sweet corn was developed specifically to eat fresh off the ear, and the blister sizes were less esteemed.

Use corn as fresh from the field as possible. Real corn fanciers insist their corn be cooked within 3 or 4 hours of the picking. Pull the husks back one at a time, remove the silks, spread the ears generously with butter, and replace the husks, tying tightly with string. Dip in water and lay in hot oven, about 400 degrees. Cook until the husks dry and start to scorch. Remove, dip in water, remove the husks, and serve. Unless a person visits the field himself there is little chance of getting hours-fresh corn. However, one can shop around and find corn no more than a day old. As corn may be kept dampened, the green of the husks is not a reliable indicator. Corn may look dry, with its husks flat-pressed, and still be excellent. If picked late on a hot day, any ear may look dry, while the flat pressing may be due to the fact it has just been dumped from the sack, fresh from the produce truck. What you really should look out for is the slick, dark-greenish appearance of corn shucks kept wet. Such corn will also show slickness and rotting where the silk emerges, and the broken butt end will be sodden rather than dry. Smell the corn. Fresh corn will have a warm, dry, sunlight fragrance.

Cut each potato in half across its greatest diameter. Using the point of a knife, cross-score the faces to about 1/4 inch. Press on a dry cloth until all possible moisture is removed. Spread with butter or bacon fat and sprinkle lightly with paprika. Rub with the thumb until the oily coating turns orange from paprika and the cross-scoring comes into view. Bake in hot oven until done. The tops will puff, crust over, and assume a beautiful golden color.

Halved, baked potatoes were favorites with people ill supplied with ovens, and that included just about all the settlers in the early days. They seldom came rolling across the plains with anything like a quarter-ton of cast-iron cookstove. Some of them owned portable army stoves, which they set up on bases of home-baked clay, and the trading posts stocked the little, one-lid Prospector's Friend. Ovens were generally purchased separately. These were made of sheet metal and had a door which required continual bending to ensure a tight fit. The oven was set on top of the stove and heated from the bottom only, although some men made their own ovens and had the stovepipe pass through them for an extra pillar of heat.

Fuel was sometimes a problem, also. Settlers living near the mountains cut and hauled good, solid pitch wood. Some of them didn't bother to cut their wood but drove around the hillsides picking up the pine knots and root crowns which had rotted from the pre-

GOLDEN BAKED POTATOES

potatoes
butter or bacon fat
paprika

historic trunks. The heavy ones were almost solid pitch, which burned like turpentine. They cast up black clouds of carbon smoke, plugging the stovepipe, but still were great lazy-man's fuel. Lignite coal was exposed in a thousand coulees gashing down to the rivers, and settlers dug their own. Few of the seams were thick enough for stand-up digging, so by the time a man got down to the solid coal he was on hands and knees, or he dug lying on his side. The coal was hauled out in sacks, by ropes fastened to saddlehorns. The slots deepened and became more dangerous as the seasons went by, but the digging went on. Out on the real, broad prairie there was often no coal, no wood, not even a sizable grove of cottonwoods. There the early fuel was buffalo chips, then cow chips, then the grubbed-out stalks of sage, and even twisted hay. Today, a "hay-burner" is a horse as distinct from an auto, but in the early West a hay-burner was just that, a stove made to burn hay. It was equipped with two horizontal fireboxes, similar to twin stovepipes, each with its door and draft, so that while a flash fire was burning itself out in one, fresh fuel could be packed in the other. The hay-burner also contained a third firebox, a conventional square one, in which heavier fuel could be burned. On top was a flat space for cooking, and an oven.

Cut potatoes in half. Cross-hatch the faces to ¼ inch with the point of a thin knife. Using splinters, fold and pin 1 slice of bacon on each. Bake under a reflector near the campfire. If you have some hot rocks to lay the potatoes on, you will find it much easier to bake them all the way through.

Lewis and Clark found the camas to be the most important vegetable of the Northwest when they made their historic journey of 1805–1806. The camas is a lily, and its bulb looks like that of a fat green onion. Pioneers called it the sweet onion—it tasted sweet and looked like an onion. Camas could be baked in quantity, dried, and stored. It could be baked, dried, and pounded into a meal. It could be boiled, peeled, and served like turnips, and it was a very acceptable substitute for pumpkin when made into pie filling. Eaten raw, the bulb of the camas is almost tasteless. Its sweet flavor develops during baking. Indians, generally the women, dug their year's supply in June and July. Western explorers found Indian villages at the best diggings, and the map of the Northwest is dotted with places named Camas Creek and Camas Prairie. The plants were easy to find. They generally had a dried flower stalk standing to a good height and a clump of broad, flattish leaves. The bulb was well-set in the ground, and the women

REFLECTOR-BAKED POTATOES

potatoes
bacon

BAKED CAMAS

1 bushel camas bulbs
water
butter
deer suet

got it by running a sharpened stick to the proper depth and prying, while at the same time giving a good, steady pull to the leaves.

The best way to prepare camas for food or storage is by pit roasting. First make sure you have genuine camas. More of that later. Sort them, discarding any which are scaly or pulpy, or which show wormholes. Put 1 bushel in a burlap sack and set it in the creek. Select a place on the bank where the ground is damp but not water-soaked, and dig a pit about 3 feet deep. Build a large fire of hardwood beside the pit. Use alder, aspen, box elder, or birch, but avoid pine or any wood likely to impart a turpentine or skunkwood flavor. When the flames have died and hot coals form, rake the fire into the hole, half filling it. Drop flat rocks on the coals one at a time. When the coals have settled and the rocks are burning hot, cover with a layer of wet mountain grass, take the sack of camas from the creek, and set it in. Step on the sack as it hisses and steams underfoot. Cover with more wet grass, or with weeds from the creek, and then with flat stones. The pit should now be almost filled. Pour in a bucket of water. When that has settled away, fill level and build a fire on top. The fire should generously cover the pit, and it should be kept going for at least 24 hours, and perhaps twice that long. As the cooking proceeds you will be aware of movement deep in the pit. It will rise, but later subside. You may notice cracks in the ground around the fire, and in the chill,

mountain morning, before the first yellow of sun, a slight mist may be seen coming from them, and clinging as if magnetized to the ground.

Let the fire die. Open the pit. The camas in the sack will be found tender, sweet, and mild in flavor. They are delicious peeled and dipped in butter. The Indians mashed them, formed them into patties, and dried them on hot rocks. These could be stored as they were or made into a meal and stored in sacks. Camas meal mixed with deer suet and baked was a concentrated food for the winter trail.

Be certain you are able to identify true camas before trying to dig any. A poisonous plant called death camas grows in much the same environment and is the chief killer of sheep on the northern range. Both true camas and death camas have large, onionlike bulbs, both are lilies with the characteristic lily or grasslike leaves, and both have their blue or white flowers in panicles or terminal racemes. However, telling them apart is not so difficult as all this sounds. The blooms look different, but as they bloom too early for this to be much help, camas diggers tell them apart by their leaves, and just by the general way they look. The death camas can be described as grasslike, while the leaves of camas more resemble the leaves of garden flags. The leaves of death camas are folded in a sharp V for most or all of the length—folded in a keel, as a botanist would say. The true camas has flat leaves. People experienced in digging camas would no more get a death camas by mistake than a gardener would pull a parsnip for carrot. If you are going to dig camas, however, have someone who knows go along the first time.

The hiker with a habit of sampling plants along the way is in most danger of eating a death camas because it looks like a nice plump onion. Play safe by bruising your onion and smelling it. If it is an onion, it will smell like an onion. Or perhaps it will be a wild leek, still edible. While on the subject, you should be aware of certain other plants. Any little wild peas are likely to be lupine, a poison. Some people might fancy gathering wild parsnips. They'd better know what they're doing because in boggy places all over the cow country there grows a similar plant, the water hemlock, whose thick root has a pronounced carrot flavor and is the deadliest root in the West. The danger from unknown berries is well known, and from mushrooms. The one other plant growing over most of the cow country which is at all likely to be consumed by humans is the milkweed, particularly the kind which grows in Utah, Arizona, Kansas, and Texas. Milkweeds when broken ooze a milky glucose substance which is tempting to children, and quite likely to be poisonous.

Boil camas until tender, peel, and skewer; alternate with lumps of deer suet on an old-fashioned Hudson's Bay Company ramrod. Salt and pepper. Have a good fire built, allow it to die to coals, rake into a doughnut form, and drive the ramrod vertically like a mast in the center. The suet will fry out, and the oil, instead of dripping into the fire, will run down the ramrod and be absorbed in the ground. As the camas are already cooked through, it is only necessary to sear them on the outside.

CAMAS SIWASH

camas bulbs
deer suet
salt and pepper
water

SOURDOUGHS & SELF-RISERS

The amounts given here will make starter for a camp of about twelve men, so you may wish to cut it proportionately. Use unbleached flour. Bleaching renders a flour sterile, getting rid of the little worms which used to add interest to mother's flour bin, but unfortunately for present purposes killing as well the natural yeasts inherited from the native wheat fields. A glance at the sack will also tell you that your bleached flour has been treated with bromine, which is quite deadly to any sort of life introduced later. Natural yeasts don't stand a chance. Even commercial yeasts are slowed down to such an extent that the big baking plants run tests on each new lot of flour to see what they're up against. The water from your tap may contain chlorine, an element closely allied to the bromine in your flour, so play safe and use rainwater, or pure water from another source, untreated.

Stir flour, water, and sugar into a medium batter. Use a receptacle made to hold three times the quantity you start out with. Camp cooks

SOURDOUGH STARTER

4 quarts flour
4 cups sugar
1 gallon warm water

105

favored kegs because they wouldn't break. Prospectors and home-steaders kept theirs in syrup buckets, but metal is best avoided. A crock is good. Unless you make your starter on a hot day, or keep it back of the kitchen range, you will probably have it up from time to time. The best way to warm it is to set a fruit jar down in the batter and pour in hot water from the teakettle. In a few hours the batter will start to work, increase in bulk, and give off a yeasty smell.

You now have a sourdough, and with luck it will be a good sour-dough. However, many varieties of yeasts can start, and you are as likely to have one which is surly in action, or gives a poor flavor. The only answer is to throw out the starter and try again, probably with another flour. Cornmeal may provide a better yeast. Some cooks added dried berries, knowing they were likely to have invisible coat-ings of natural yeast. Some added wine, alcohol lower than 13 per-cent, knowing that wine yeasts will exist for years in suspended ani-mation.

With all this difficulty why not just use a pinch of commercial yeast? Because then it would be a yeast starter and not a sourdough starter. Sourdough breads and pancakes taste different. Their batter lacks the puff and life of commercial yeast, but it is long on sourness, or acid. To neutralize the acid, and give added life to the batter, soda is added a short time before it is put in the oven. Soda and acid will generate carbon dioxide, just like a baking powder. Hence the true, natural sourdough product owes its lightness to both. The amount of soda needed for the various recipes will be indicated, but as a general guide add 1 teaspoon for each 4 cups (or each pound) of flour used in the dough.

When the sourdough gets to working full-steam, store it in a cool place. Not a cold place, just cool. It shouldn't boil over the crock, nor should it stop working. It should be just right. You may now dip from it as a yeast for pancakes, biscuits, or bread. Try not to use more than two-thirds at any time. As soon as some is taken out, replace that same amount with new flour, water, and sugar.

Because a sourdough starter once developed might never be produced again, the frontier cook went to great lengths protecting it. The notorious fluctuations in temperature common at high altitudes presented his greatest problem. He might roll along with the sun beating down on his wagon, raising the temperature under the canvas to more than 100 degrees, and then see it drop down to freezing that same night. One extreme was as great a danger as the other. At high temperatures, particularly in a jouncing wagon, the dough would boil over and work itself stale; and the cold would paralyze it. Cooks cooled their sourdough kegs by laying wet gunnysacks over them, and many a night, when a blizzard swept the plains, they wrapped their kegs in their own blanket while they themselves sat shivering. They took their kegs to bed with them, and as a last resort they built campfires, raked the coals away, and set the keg on the warmed place with a tarp draped over it. Cooks kept their favorite starters going for years, but it wasn't easy.

Prospectors, trappers, and bachelor farmers could not stay with their sourdough starters as the camp cooks did. Winter and summer, they might be gone all day, or several days, even weeks. Did they give up on sourdoughs and cook self-risers with baking powder? Not at all. They found that starter made into a thin batter could be poured out on cheesecloth over old newspaper and dried in the sun. Once hard and stored in a cool place, pieces could be taken out and used like regular dry yeast. It kept even better in winter. Taken at the peak of activity, the starter was poured out and frozen. Kept frozen, pieces could be broken with a hammer, its activity unimpaired when thawed. In fact, some cooks claimed their frozen starter worked even better. There is little need today for home drying of yeast, but many cooks store their starter in the deep freeze. Not in the refrigerator! Starter can stand the decisive action, but three or four days in a refrigerator seem to leave it drugged, hopelessly impaired.

Not all pioneer starters were made by natural fermentation. Many of the wagon immigrants arrived carrying their own yeast, or starter, from back East, and even from the old country. Bakers sent to far places for favorite strains of yeast, as did the brewers. A yeast starter is easier to make. Mix the ingredients, get them to working, and store in a cool place. Unbleached flour is best, but it is not necessary as in the case of natural sourdough.

About 1 hour before baking time transfer the sourdough starter from the crock to a mixing bowl. Add the flour, salt, shortening, and enough water to form a heavy batter. Cover, let rise. If you intend to bake your biscuits on an open fire, you will need Dutch ovens, which should be heated well beforehand. Mix the soda and sugar together. This will help it stir evenly through the batter. Sprinkle over the batter and beat for at least 5 minutes. Turn out on a heavily floured board, pat flat, cut in circles about 4 inches across. Add bacon grease in good quantity to the Dutch ovens. Most camp cooks liked to have at least 1/4 inch of hot melted grease. Put the biscuits to bake. Because of the very soft dough they will handle like doughnuts. If an open fire is used, cover and put a shovelful of hot coals on each lid. If an oven is used, no cover is necessary, but the oven should be good and hot,

YEAST STARTER

1 quart flour
1 cake yeast
1 cup sugar
1 1/2 quarts water

CHUCKWAGON SOURDOUGH BISCUITS

2 quarts sourdough starter
water
4 quarts flour
4 teaspoons soda
2 tablespoons salt
1/2 cup sugar
1/2 cup shortening
bacon grease

109

about 400 degrees. Twenty-five minutes in an oven should be enough. Cooking over an open fire is more difficult. It is generally a good idea to take the Dutch oven off the fire as soon as the smell of browning crust can be detected and let the baking proceed from the heat of the iron and the coals on top.

YEAST STARTER BISCUITS

If you make your biscuits with a yeast starter instead of the natural sourdough, the chances are soda will not be required. It all depends on how much bounce there is in the yeast. Proceed exactly as with Chuckwagon Sourdoughs up to the final beating. If the batter is nice and bubbly at that time, add the sugar but not the soda. However, if you get a sour smell rather than a live yeast smell, and nothing much seems to be happening, add the soda. Yeasts are living things and hence have their moods and temperaments. Not even the most experienced camp cook had the predictable results with starter breads they had with self-risers. But he felt, and his men did too, that the delectable quality of success more than compensated for an occasional failure.

Into a large bowl mix half the flour and the other dry ingredients. Pour in the bacon grease and work thoroughly with the fingers. When this has been blended, pour in the yeast starter—for some reason sourdough starter never works so well in bread as in biscuits—the water, warmed, and the canned milk. Stir and allow to stand in a moderately warm place. After 1 or 2 hours, when it has worked to double its size and is all bubbly, beat, add the remaining flour—most of it, all of it, or a little more, as required—to form a sticky dough. Mix and then knead until smooth. Form into a large ball, pat down, wet the surface, and cover with a dry cloth. If the room is cool, put several thicknesses of cloth, even a blanket, over the mixing bowl. Fermentation is a fire of sorts, producing its own warmth, and generally it is well to preserve it.

Allow the dough to double again in size. Knead, adding flour as needed to prevent it hanging unduly to the hands. Cut into loaf-size pieces and knead some more. At this stage the dough should be resilient and a joy to work with. "It should be," said one old camp cook, "like the breasts of a voluptuous woman." Ah, yes. Knead and mix and have pleasure with the good live dough in your hands. Kneading the loaves is the most important step in the bread-making process. Children given bits of dough to mix into baby loaves generally make the best bread because they keep at it, and keep at it. As a

BREAD

1 quart yeast starter
3 rounded tablespoons salt
10 pounds unbleached flour
1 cup bacon grease
2 quarts water
1 cup sugar
2 tall cans milk

guide, holding within realistic limits, mix each loaf for 5 minutes. When the mixing is done, the dough should half fill the loaf pan, which is greased waiting to receive it.

Bake in a medium-hot oven, about 350 degrees, for 45 minutes, more or less, depending on the size of the loaf. The above recipe will work very well with yeast. Two yeast cakes or 2 tablespoons of dry yeast will substitute for 1 quart of starter. Dry milk can be substituted for canned milk. Fresh whole milk, if used, should be scalded. Bleached flour will substitute for unbleached, but because of the chemicals you may find your yeast slowed. The chemicals prevent worms from hatching. Few unbleached flours have any worms today, but if you wish to use one of them and are worried about various larvae hatching, store the flour in your deep freeze. Even if some wildlife does develop, it is better for you than daily dosages of bromine.

The sourdough starter already given is fine for pancakes, but some westerners preferred a cornmeal type. Mix unbleached flour, cornmeal, sugar, and enough rainwater to make a medium batter. Cover with a dish towel and set in the sun. This should start to work in about 5 hours. When fermentation can be smelled, put the starter in a cool place.

The night before add flour, cornmeal, sugar, and enough water to make a batter. Put this right into the starter crock. You can add more of the ingredients in the same proportion, or less. However much batter you want for breakfast, that's what you add to the starter. Next morning all should be working at a low level, so pour out an amount equal to what was added the night before. Set the remaining starter back in storage and proceed with the batter. To this add eggs, canned milk, water, and soda. Beat hard. If you like thin pancakes—and western pancakes were generally thin—add water to make a thin batter. If you like pancakes with a sourish taste—and those, too, were the favorites—go easy on the soda. Or leave out the soda altogether. Fry on a heavy iron griddle, using plenty of butter or bacon grease.

If you prefer regular white flour pancakes, leave out the cornmeal after the original setting of sourdough. Use all white flour instead. Or you can use a mixture of white flour and buckwheat or white flour and farina, giving different flavors and textures. It is best to make a

SOURDOUGH PANCAKES

PART 1
1 cup flour
1 cup cornmeal
2 tablespoons sugar
water

PART 2
2 cups flour
1 teaspoon baking soda
1 cup cornmeal
1/3 cup sugar
1/3 teaspoon salt
3 eggs
water
1 cup canned milk

thin gruel of the farina if it is used. Some cooks also boiled their corn-meal before adding, and with superb results.

Mix the ingredients thoroughly. Pack in a stout sack if it is to be carried camping, or in a canister if used in the kitchen.

Open the sack of self-rising flour. Form a depression by pushing the fist down hard. Pour in the warmed bacon fat. Mix with the tips of the fingers until the fat has spread as far as it cares to. This will be a volume of about 2 cups in size. Make a depression in the oil-filled flour. Pour in the water. It will move rapidly until it reaches the dry flour, where it will stop. Mix until the proper dough is formed. Make a ball of the dough and lift it out. Tie the sack and suspend it from a beam of the cabin, the tent ridge, or a limb where it will be out of the reach of pack rats. Wire is better for this than rope. Put bacon to fry in a Dutch oven. Press the dough flat and cut in circles with a tin cup, or form into balls. Drop in hot grease. Cover. If the Dutch oven is sitting

SELF-RISING FLOUR

10 pounds flour
4 cups sugar
1 cup cream of tartar
1/3 cup salt
baking powder
3 cups powdered milk

PROSPECTOR'S BISCUITS

self-rising flour
1 cup water
2 tablespoons bacon grease

115

directly on the coals, move it. Some cooks elevate the oven on stones; others rake the coals away and place it on the hot earth. Inside 5 minutes the good smell of baking biscuits should reach you. If it doesn't, peek inside and see how things are doing. If the oven is of heavy iron and starts out hot enough to fry bacon, no trouble should be experienced, though a cold wind may cause difficulty. Wind rather than cold is the enemy of the campfire cook. When the wind is bad, try leaning several burning sticks against the Dutch oven so their heat will be carried around and over it. Biscuits in a Dutch oven, being covered, and pulling heat readily from the iron where ample amounts are in storage, should bake in less time than in a regular oven—under ideal conditions in as little as 8 minutes.

The biscuit dough of the previous recipe can be used to make dumplings if desired. Merely float the biscuits on top of the stew, put an extra-large heap of coals on the cover, and they will be dumplings, browned on top. The common quick Camp Dumplings are made without shortening, however. Merely mix water with self-rising flour to form a sticky dough and spoon this into the boiling liquid, dipping the spoon each time so it will continue to work cleanly. Cover and allow from 10 to 15 minutes. No coals on the lid are required.

CAMP DUMPLINGS

self-rising flour
water

116

When there is no meat for the pot, satisfactory dumplings can still be made. Put water to boil with a generous helping of bacon grease, salt pork grease, or even lard. The grease will form a thick, white gravy around the dumplings when they are cooked, giving the flavor of a rich stew. A few wild onions and young leaves of mountain sorrel added to the boiling water will help give flavor.

HARD-TIME STEW

camp dumplings
boiling water
bacon grease
wild onions and mountain sorrel
   leaves, optional

Mix the dry ingredients thoroughly and add enough water, little by little, to form a stiff dough. Bake like camp biscuits, or form into ribbons, wrap around a stick, and bake over a fire.

BANNOCK

2 cups flour
1 rounded teaspoon
   baking powder
1/2 teaspoon salt
cold water

117

Frying-Pan Bread

1 cup flour
1/4 cup sugar
1/2 cup cornmeal
1 rounded teaspoon
 baking powder
bacon or salt pork
water

Ash Cakes

2 cups flour
1/2 cup farina
1 rounded teaspoon
 baking powder
6 strips bacon or salt pork
water

Boil the cornmeal using enough water to make a thin mush. Cool. Mix the other dry ingredients, add to the mush, form a dough, knead and press flat, round, and about the size of your frying pan. Fry out a few strips of bacon or salt pork, then remove, leaving the hot oil in the pan. Carefully fit in the dough—it will be quite tender because of the cornmeal—lay the bacon or salt pork on the top, cover, and bake at a slow heat for about 8 minutes.

This is a good emergency bread if you have run out of baking powder. In that event, add a little extra cornmeal. The bread will be quite tender without leavening.

Mix the flour and baking powder and add enough water to make a tough dough. Divide into six portions and flatten out, pressing between the hands. Lay a strip of bacon or salt pork on each and form roll-ups. Pat with water and roll in farina. Press the farina into the outside, pat again with water, and repeat. Lay in hot ashes, rake a thick coating of ashes over the top and finally some smoldering sticks. Allow to bake 1/2 hour or so. Whenever flames appear, or when the strong smell of burning grease arises, this will mean that the fat pork has fried out and your Ash Cakes are probably done. On the other hand, they offer a great latitude. Some campers bury their morning

Ash Cakes the night before and arise to find them hot and succulent inside their hard shell of farina.

Flour, water, and salt baked on a griddle or in the ashes makes a Bannock of sorts. Without leavening, it comes out just barely chewable, and after being carried for one or two days will turn hard as some soft stone, such as shale. Pioneers with no provisions but flour and salt devised a number of ways to make their Doughgods more chewable. The batter could be allowed to ferment, but lacking soda it was likely to taste pretty bad. Taking a page from the Indians' book, some of them made a meal of pounded dried serviceberries and mixed this in to vary the solid brick of baked flour. In the winter, when camped near the snow line, a flour dough can be buried in a snowbank and when almost frozen, mixed with a good helping of snow. The snow crystals, baking out, will leave holes which are almost like the gas holes of baking powder.

DOUGHGODS

flour
water
salt

Suet Dumplings

2 cups flour
1/2 teaspoon salt
1/4 pound suet
water

Corn Doughgods
or Quick & Greasy

1 quart flour
4 tablespoons baking powder
1 quart cornmeal
1 cup shortening
1 tablespoon salt
1 cup sugar, optional
water

Pound the suet to a pulp. When it is an oily mass held together, more or less, by its webbing of tissues, mix in the flour and salt. Add a few drops of water to form a dough. Mix for at least 10 minutes, first with the hands and then with a wooden paddle. A camp hatchet is very good for the purpose. Mix until the dough is smooth-shiny and plastic as clay. Form into 1½-inch-size balls and drop into stew. Cover and cook slowly for ½ hour. Suet Dumplings, made without leavening or eggs, and cooked in a rich venison stew, are as good as any dumpling made.

Fry bacon or salt pork. Keep frying until there is enough for everybody. By that time the pan, or pans, should contain ½ to 1 inch of hot grease. Dip out a cupful of this to cool and leave the rest in the pan, hot. Mix grease, flour, cornmeal, salt, and baking powder. The sugar is optional. Add water and stir to make a heavy batter. Spoon this immediately into the hot grease, which should be in sufficient quantity to bubble up, halfway floating the Doughgods. Turn them over when brown. More bacon and salt pork can be fried at the same time, the process to go on until everyone is fed. A luxury touch, the Corn Doughgods may be dipped in sugar as dessert.

DESSERTS

Bring the apples to boil, remove from heat, add the sugar, grate in the nutmegs, sprinkle on the cinnamon, cover, and set aside. Proceed with the crust. The cook who holds too exactly to measurements will never be a first-rate pie maker. Flour is ground to varying degrees of fineness, some kinds pack more solidly than others, and a great deal depends on the eye of the cook. Mix the 2 quarts of flour and the salt, add 2 cups of lard. Mix with fingertips, adding more lard until the mixture hangs together when squeezed but easily breaks apart. Add water little by little until the crust can be rolled and lifted. For a western style of Dried Apple Pie, don't make any great point of rolling a thin piecrust, or rolling one with almost no water. It was made to be eaten by hand rather than fork.

Oh yes, westerners know how to eat pie with forks. But pie was made to be taken up in the fingers, solidly and reliably in one piece, and so eaten if desired.

DRIED APPLE PIE

2 quarts flour
1 quart sugar
2 1/2 cups lard
2 nutmegs
1 rounded teaspoon salt
1 teaspoon cinnamon
1 pound dried apples
1/2 cup flour
1 quart water
salt

123

Roll out on a well-floured board. Drape the crust over the tins, press down, and cut to size. It is better to use a knife and cut the dough rather than pinch it off. Cutting will leave a thicker undamaged rim of crust, the better to hold together when cut into pieces. Be sure there are no breaks in the crust or else the juice will run under and glue it to the tin.

The dried apples, which now have been 1 hour or so off the stove, should be almost cold. Stir in about ½ cup of flour. Fill the crusts quite full, but don't heap as you do when using fresh apples. Dried apples which have been brought to a boil 1 hour beforehand will thereafter neither increase nor decrease much in bulk. Place on the top crusts. Cut again, then pinch together, bringing the dough up in a ridge rather than pinching it down against the rim. Cut vents for the steam to escape, but as few as possible. Try making one hole in the exact center and one for each segment you intend to cut it into. The most eye-appealing piece of pie is an exact one-fifth. Cut a five-pointed star in the middle and an opening halfway down each radius, then when the pie is cut in five pieces, each will have a decoration in its center and its tip will be unbroken. Some cooks paint their pies with condensed milk and sprinkle them with sugar for gloss and added flavor. Bake in a hot oven for about 45 minutes. Very successful camp pies can be baked in a Dutch oven.

Remove the salt and discoloration from the bacon grease by pouring the warm—not hot—grease into boiling water. When the water grows cold, the grease can be lifted from the top. Proceed as with Dried Apple Pie but use these ingredients, which will better overcome the bacon flavor.

BACON-GREASE PIE

2 quarts flour
2 1/2 cups bacon grease
water
1 pound dried apples or peaches
2 tablespoons vinegar
1 quart sugar
1/2 cup flour
1/2 teaspoon nutmeg
1/2 teaspoon cinnamon
1/4 teaspoon cloves

125

WILDCAT PIE
OR VINEGAR PIE

pastry dough
1/2 cup vinegar
1/2 pound suet
flour as needed
1 cup water
1 cup sugar
dried peaches, optional

Chop the suet and fry out. Discard the crackling. Add water and bring to a boil. Add the vinegar. Stir in flour slowly, creaming to form a paste. Add sugar and pour into a dough-lined pie tin. Cover with dough, cut numerous openings for escaping steam, sprinkle sugar over the top, and bake until the crust is crisp and brown. The result is surprisingly like a fruit pie.

In the Old West, visitors at camps where Vinegar Pie was made (not by choice but because nothing else for a pie was available) asked for the recipe and refused to believe the cook when he told them there was nothing in the filling except suet, sugar, water, and vinegar. They thought there was a secret ingredient. Not so. The flavor came from sugar, bubbling and caramelizing through holes in the crust, and from the vinegar which substituted for fruit acid. If the cook had a few leftover dried peaches, he might cut them small and mix them in to heighten the illusion of fruit in his Vinegar Pie.

FRIED PEACH PIE

pastry dough
1 quart sugar
1 pound dried peaches
1 quart water
1 nutmeg
1/2 cup flour

Fried Peach Pie was a favorite of the outdoor cooks when they wanted pie and had no oven, not even a Dutch oven, to bake one in.

Chop the peaches to about ½-inch size and put to boil with sugar and grated nutmeg. The quart of water is only approximate because dried peaches vary greatly in water content, some being soft enough to eat straight while some are as dry as a mummy's ear. Boil gently for a few minutes and set off the fire to cool. Using a trifle more flour than you would for a pie—and more water—roll out a crust. Cut in circles using an 8- or 9-inch empty can. Place each circle of dough in a steep-sided bowl where it will sag and form a receptacle. Dip in 1 cup of fruit—more or less depending on what the dough will easily hold. Pinch the edges together and form a pastie shell. Flatten gently on a floured board. Steam vents pose a problem if the pie is to be fried on both sides. Some cooks cut them down the spine where the dough folds over. Perhaps the best way is to cut vents on the top only and fry under a lid on which a few hot coals were sprinkled, and not turn at all. Bake until the crust is brittle and caramelized peach juice has formed around the edge.

Fill a deep bucket or a large syrup can two-thirds to the top with water and set to boil. Select a sack of tight cotton material and drop a clean, smooth stone in the bottom. The stone will narrow the sack to any desired diameter, and hence its size is optional. Make a hoop slightly larger than the stone to open the top of the sack. Set down in cold water, wet all the way to the hoop, lift, hang up, and dust the inside with self-rising flour. Immerse again, and repeat, building up a layer of dough inside the sack. When the dough is 1 inch thick, more or less, make a mixture of the fruits, suet, sugar, spices, and flour. Pour in. Remove the hoop and tie the top. Set in boiling water and cook slowly for 6 hours or more. Lift out and set in the creek, the spring, or the coldest water you can find. After 1 or 2 hours the sack can be peeled away, leaving the pudding firmly encased in dough, to be spooned up or sliced as desired. Just as Son-of-a-Bitch-in-a-Sack with meat can be called a cowboy's Haggis, this is the cowboy's Plum Pudding.

SON-OF-A-BITCH-IN-A-SACK II

2 pounds self-rising flour
1 pound sugar
6 pounds dried fruits
1 pound suet
1 teaspoon nutmeg
1/2 teaspoon cinnamon
water
1/2 cup plain flour

SHEEP SHEARER'S DELIGHT
OR DIRTY GEORGE

1 loaf bread, sliced
1/2 cup molasses
butter to spread
1/2 cup corn syrup
1 quart sheep's milk

Unlike cowboys who got all their milk from cans because they wouldn't sink to taking supper away from a calf, sheep shearers were not above robbing a lamb of its next meal, and while a mother ewe was on the floor being sheared was a good time to do it. A cook for a gang of sheep shearers hence had fresh milk for the asking. One of the things he made was this excellent bread pudding.

Spread the sliced bread with butter on both sides, arrange in a pan, and cover with a mixture of milk, molasses, and syrup. Bake in a slow oven about 2 hours, stirring gently from time to time and adding milk if needed. Serve with cold milk to which a few drops of vanilla have been added.

When made with canned milk, Sheep Shearer's Delight went by the name of Dirty George, but whether in honor of some cook by that name, or because of its blotchy gray-brown appearance, the author does not know. In winter some cooks, as a treat, served Dirty George with a topping of snow-whipped canned milk. Pour a can of sweetened condensed milk into a crockery bowl and set outside when the temperature is below zero. When the milk is bladed with ice, stir in a handful of loose, crisp snow and beat until light. An excellent flavoring for this may be made by boiling sweetened leftover coffee until thick and adding a few drops of vanilla.

COFFEE

In the Old West, the real Old West, coffee came in a gunnysack, green, and had to be roasted before use. The roasting was generally performed in a long-armed skillet, under a lid, and the beans kept in motion like popcorn. It is an exacting job to roast coffee without scorching it, so scorched was how much of it went to the pot. Later the firm of Arbuckle Brothers got the idea of roasting coffee before-hand and packing it in convenient 1-pound paper bags. Arbuckle's coffee was such a success in the West that cowboys came to think of Arbuckle and coffee as meaning the same thing. Like Stetson and Colt, the name was still so western that when Fatty Arbuckle started making motion pictures, the cow country accepted him as its own. Later when Fatty stood trial on a particularly repellent morals charge, the West felt sold out, and a picture house in Wyoming which had the effrontery to show one of his comedies was actually laid waste by an angry mob armed with six-shooters and lariat ropes.

CAMP COFFEE

1/3 pound coffee
3 quarts water

131

Although the Arbuckle brothers relieved cooks of coffee roasting, the beans still had to be ground. Nearly all chuckwagons had a coffee grinder attached, generally inside where it could be reached from the ground out back, but not where it ran the risk of being torn off when the wagon had to be gee-hawed across bushy creek bottoms. Most cooks put through an entire pound sack of coffee at one time, requiring 640 turns of the crank. With coffee served at three meals, and from dark to dawn for the night herders, it was a lucky cook who saw one cranking carry him through 24 hours. Spavined old cattlemen wintering in town always told how much better the coffee used to be. And indeed it was. Coffee is always better when ground from the whole bean right beside the pot.

Use the best water available. Avoid alkali water, and deep well water. The terrible coffee one finds served in many western towns owes its taste to the hard water from deep wells. Try to make your coffee from rainwater or from snow-fed mountain streams. For Camp Coffee the best pot is an iron one of at least 1-gallon size. Be sure it is clean. Mud is excellent for cleaning the inside of a coffeepot. Use good fresh clay. Clay always contains enough sand to give it a tooth, while the kaolin emulsifies and carries off the rancid oils. Today's scouring powders leave behind a taste of cheap perfume more objectionable than the old coffee coatings they take away.

When the pot is clean, and smells clean, fill three-quarters of the way with cold water. Grind the coffee and dump on the water where most of it will float. Set the pot on the fire, either on a grate or on hot ashes surrounded by coals. Do not cover. Keep close watch. Stir when the first big bubbles arise to keep from boiling over the sides. When the thick, brown foam stops and a brisk boiling follows it, set the pot in a cooler place. It can be put on a rock heated for the purpose or on the ground, but make sure the hot light of the fire strikes it. This will keep it steeping, but from the sides rather than the bottom. Settle with a cup of cold water and serve.

Keep your coffee just below boiling point and it will be good for hours. Camp Coffee was kept hot all night for the herders; more water and fresh-ground coffee were added, new made on old, and still it remained good. The secret is never to allow the pot to cool. Similarly, coffee stood on the backs of stoves in numberless ranch kitchens with fine results, enjoyed by those who came in from the cold. However, once it cools, the heat required to bring it around again will surely scorch the sediments and oily coatings always present, and give it that ugly reheated-coffee taste.

To keep Camp Coffee hot, fill a 5-gallon can one-quarter full of dirt and set it on the coals. Get it hot enough so the roots, twigs, and fragments of leaves smoke out and turn to ash. The dirt will retain its

heat long after the fire has died beneath it. When leaving camp set the coffeepot down inside where it will be protected from the breeze. On cold or windy days a gold-pan or similar cover can be put on top. Such a dirt container will substitute also for a double boiler. This method can also be used for Hunter's Coffee on page 136.

Few prospectors owned coffee mills, or at least few carried mills around on their pack animals. Coffee beans, however, could be crushed very easily if they were heated first. Heating makes them almost like raisins—that is, soft as raisins although not so tough—inside a thin, shell-like coating.

Heat the beans in a frying pan, shaking constantly. You may detect a scorched smell, but this won't mean you have burned them. The smell will probably come from a minute amount of coffee oil that coats and smokes up from the metal. When hot and soft, pour the beans in a mortar and crush. There will be some coffee powder, but mostly the beans will be flattened, and you'll have to scrape them off the bottom of the mortar. Put a quart of creek water on the fire and add the coffee. Bring to a boil, cover, and steep in the shining heat of the fire. Coffee from mashed rather than ground beans will take longer to steep, but due to the fresh roast it may be the best coffee you ever made.

PROSPECTOR'S COFFEE

2/3 cup coffee beans
1 quart water

Hunter's Coffee

1 cup ground coffee
1 tall can milk
2/3 quart water
2 tablespoons butter
sugar

Put the coffee to boiling. Punch a hole in a can of milk and set it on a rock near the fire, where it will heat. After the coffee has steeped until it has become very strong, and bubbles rise from the hole in the can of milk, pour the coffee in another pot, add the milk, and stir in the butter. Even people who do not ordinarily take sugar in their coffee will probably take a spoonful or two in a cup of this. It is particularly good on cold, wet autumn mornings to set a hunter off into the woods. A similar coffee, made in western saloons, was called Coffee Boston and was a favorite with gamblers and others who had extended themselves the night before.

Bartender's Coffee Boston

strong coffee
medium cream
butter
sugar

Heat a heavy porcelain cup on the stove until too hot to pick up. Using a cloth, and with the cloth left around it, put the cup on the bar and fill it almost halfway with thin cream. When the handle is cool enough to take hold of, fill the cup with hot, strong coffee, add a small lump of butter, and serve with sugar at hand.

136

WINES & FANCIES

You will need two crocks 6 to 10 gallons in size and a 5-gallon white oak keg. Pick the chokecherries when they are black-ripe in late August or September. Or pick them later when they have been touched by frost, and, according to some, improved and sweetened thereby. Dump the berries into a large tub and wash in a stream of cold water. Allow the water to overflow the tub and carry off twigs and leaves.

Lift the berries a few at a time and crush. Any method which breaks the skin will be satisfactory. They are small and tough-skinned, so many will escape no matter what the method. After crushing, place in one of the crocks, add 2 gallons of water, 1 pound of sugar, and the yeast cake. Cover, and allow to stand for 1 day at about 70 degrees. By that time fermentation will be active and the pulped berries threatening to overflow the crock. Lift the dryish pulp to the second crock. Strain the berries from the liquid below and add

CHOKECHERRY WINE

5 gallons ripe chokecherries
11 pounds sugar
yeast cake
water as needed

137

them also. Add 1 pound of sugar and 1 gallon of water to the pulp and strained berries. Stir and allow the fermentation to proceed. You will now have about 1½ gallons of deep red juice. Pour into the keg. Add 1 pound of sugar, rock the keg until the sugar is dissolved, cork lightly, and cover with a damp, clean burlap sack.

Wait 1 day. Again lift the pulp and strain out the berries, returning to the first crock. Add 1 gallon of water and 1 pound of sugar. Stir. Add the juice to that already in the keg. Add 1 pound of sugar and mix as before. Wait 1 more day.

Now on the third day, you will be finished with the berries. Strain off what juice you can and squeeze the rest. This can be done either with a wine press or a jelly sack. Add to the first two days' strainings in the keg. Stir in the remainder of the 11 pounds of sugar—in this case, unless arithmetic failed, 6 pounds. The keg should be about three-quarters full. Add water until 1 inch from the hole, cork lightly, cover with the damp sack, and wait.

Fermentation will go on briskly for a few days and subside, but a couple of months may pass before you will be able to cork the keg tightly. Do so, wait another month, then open the keg and sample the contents. If clear, and the dregs all at the bottom, decant the wine and bottle, or transfer it to another keg. If you have only one keg, and wish nevertheless to recask your wine, decant it into a crock, wash the keg with hot water, and return the wine to it.

In recasking wine rather than bottling it, you will have a small problem. The dregs, evaporation, and the loss through fermentation will leave the keg short at least 2 quarts, and it will have to be full. Many wine-makers have a gallon of wine set in a jug for addition at this time. Lacking such foresight, add alcohol and water in a 12 percent mixture or better. If you add water alone, you will weaken the wine and either start it to fermenting again or risk it spoiling. Wine too weak often turns to vinegar.

Allow to age when bottled or recasked. Chokecherry Wine made one year is excellent the next. Wine started in September is good by Christmas, but another two or three months will improve it a great deal.

Dessert Chokecherry Wine

12 pounds sugar
6 to 8 gallons ripe chokecherries
yeast cake
water as needed
drinking alcohol

For 5 gallons of sweet dessert wine resembling port, use 12 pounds of sugar and 6 to 8 gallons of ripe chokecherries—the riper the better. When the fermentation in the keg subsides, add alcohol in some relatively tasteless form—vodka will be fine—to bring the percentage up to around 18 percent. The wine will already be about 11 percent, so a pencil and paper is called for. Remember that a proof is not the same as a percent. Eighty-proof is 40 percent. "Pure grain alcohol" is not 100 percent either. It is generally about 90 percent, or 180-proof. If you use alcohol to fortify your wine, be certain it is drinking alcohol. Alcohol is often high-graded, as the miners say, from a commercial lab, so make sure.

Dry, Claret-Type Chokecherry Wine

8 to 9 pounds sugar
4 gallons ripe chokecherries
yeast cake
water as needed

For 5 gallons of red wine resembling a claret, use 8 to 9 pounds of sugar and cut the amount of berries to about 4 gallons. Proceed as in recipe above.

140

Best wishes for your Christmas
Is all you get from me,
'Cause I aint no Santa Claus —
Don't own no Christmas tree.

But if wishes was health and money,
I'd fill your buck-skin poke,
Your doctor would go hungry
An' you never would be broke.

Bright Red Chokecherry Wine

4 gallons red chokecherries
water as needed
brandy or grain alcohol
1 cup pounded chokecherry pits
8 pounds sugar
yeast cake

Pick the chokecherries early when they are red, just turning ripe. Heat in warm water to soften. Crush and place in a crock with a gallon of warm water. Add 1 pound of sugar and a yeast cake. Decant the juice after a day and put the juice thus gained in a 5-gallon keg. Add 1 pound of sugar to the keg, mix, cork lightly, and cover with a clean, damp burlap bag. Add 1 gallon of water to the berries, 1 pound of sugar, and let work another day. Press out the juice, discard the berries. Add the juice to that already in the keg, stir in the remainder of the 8 pounds of sugar, fill with water to the 4½ gallon point, cork lightly, cover as before, and allow to work for several days. Keep close watch and when the fermentation starts to subside but the wine is still sweet, add brandy or alcohol in sufficient quantity to kill the fermentation. Cork tightly and leave for about 6 weeks. In that time the wine should be a clear scarlet and have the marked flavor of maraschino cherries. Recask, filling the keg to the cork with a 20 percent mixture of alcohol and water, perhaps in the form of brandy or vodka mixed with water one-for-one. A cupful of cracked chokecherry stones will increase the cherry flavor.

Stem and mash the raspberries, crush, add vinegar, and let stand overnight. Strain, add water to the pulp, stir, allow to stand for a while, then press through a cloth to get all the juice. Add sugar to the juice, bring to a boil, and bottle.

This made an excellent drink. It was also a winter treat poured over packed balls of very cold snow.

RASPBERRY SHRUB

1 gallon wild raspberries
2 pounds sugar
1 pint vinegar
1 pint water

Crush the ripe berries, add the other ingredients, and simmer very gently for 30 minutes. Let stand overnight.

BUFFALOBERRY RELISH

1 quart buffaloberries
1 pint vinegar
2 dozen wild onions
1 teaspoon dry mustard
1/8 teaspoon cayenne
1/2 cup sugar
2 tablespoons salt

CHOKECHERRY SYRUP

5 pounds chokecherries
5 pounds sugar
1/2 cup vinegar

CORNCOB SYRUP

tub of dry corncobs
5 pounds sugar
water

Boil the chokecherries and syrup as for jelly-making, squeeze out all the juice possible, add the vinegar, boil until it coats a spoon, and store in sterilized glass jars. Chokecherries will not jell without the addition of pectin, or as a mixture half-and-half with crab apples, so the result will be a heavy syrup, much favored for use on biscuits.

Scour the family washtub with clean, bright sand until the last traces of soap and scum have been removed. Set on the kitchen range one-third full of cold water, and put in as many dry corncobs as it will hold. Boil slowly. Every couple of hours stir enough so hot steaming cobs will be on top and fresh ones go to the bottom. After 10 or 12 hours remove the cobs, allow them to drain, and discard. Add sugar and boil until you obtain a medium syrup. The sap from cobs is a good substitute for maple. This is not to claim that one raised in the sugarbush couldn't instantly tell the difference, only that the excellence of the products are comparable.

This photograph was taken in 1895 at a roundup camp on lower Eagle Creek, Chouteau County, Montana. The cook is "Shankmeat" Barrett; shown seated beside the cook with his back against the rear wagon wheel is Mose Tingley, whose father and uncle, cattle barons of the Judith Basin and Big Sandy ranges, sent Charlie Russell away to art school. At the far right is Bertrand W. Sinclair, who had ridden over from beyond the Little Rockies on a horse wearing the Fiddleback brand and thereupon became known as "The Fiddleback Kid." Later he took to bartending, and next story writing. Of all western novelists known to this writer only Sinclair and Walt Coburn had been real, honest-to-God cowboys, and Sinclair was the honest-to-godder of the two.

146

ILLUSTRATIONS

BY CHARLIE RUSSELL

147

Rawhide Rawlins, courtesy Montana Historical Society, Helena, Montana, Mackay Collection (page 89).

Buffalo Hunter, courtesy *Great Falls Tribune* (page 91).

Mountains and Plains Seemed to Stimulate a Man's Imagination, courtesy Montana Historical Society, Helena, Montana, Mackay Collection (page 92).

The Stage Robber, courtesy *Great Falls Tribune* (page 98).

Flathead Squaw and Papoose, courtesy *Great Falls Tribune* (page 104).

The Bull Whacker, courtesy *Great Falls Tribune* (page 114).

Wood Hawk, courtesy *Great Falls Tribune* (page 116).

Like a Flash They Turned, courtesy Montana Historical Society, Helena, Montana, Mackay Collection (page 121).

Halfbreed Trader, courtesy *Great Falls Tribune* (page 122).

Old Macheers Saddle with Texas Tree, courtesy Bradley M. Hamlett, Sun River, Montana (page 125).

Young Sioux Squaw, courtesy *Great Falls Tribune* (page 127).

The Prospector, courtesy *Great Falls Tribune* (page 134).

Best Wishes for Your Christmas, courtesy Montana Historical Society, Helena, Montana (page 141).

Mosquito Season in Cascade, courtesy Montana Historical Society, Helena, Montana, gift of Mrs. Charles L. Sheridan (page 145).

All other illustrations throughout the book are courtesy of the *Great Falls Tribune,* Great Falls, Montana.

FAMILY RECIPES